THERE ARE PLACES I'LL REMEMBER

This book is dedicated to the late Alf Bicknell, Beatles chauffeur from 1964 to 1966. Paul McCartney said of Alf, "Not everyone you meet is loyal, not everybody is someone you can trust, and not everyone is a likeable person, but Alf scored easily on all three points." Alf sadly passed away in 2004. I was privileged to know him as a friend.

ACKNOWLEDGEMENTS I wish to thank the following who have all made helpful contributions to this book and whose input is very much appreciated. Also to those who made their collection of ticket stubs, posters and private photographs available for inclusion. I list them in random order in the knowledge that no doubt I have unintentionally omitted some people: David Brown, Tony Booth, Jim Irlam, Harry Prytherch, Roger Shone, Bill Slater, Adrian Knight, Patrick Dunleavy, Bob Evans, David Bedford, Spencer Leigh, Billy Halliday, Chris Hannah, Mary Newton, Alec Paton, Maurice Williams, Charlie Roberts, Bobby Scott, Eric Woolley, Elly Roberts and Harry Thomas.

The review on the back cover was written by Brad Howard, Editor of *The World Beatles Forum Magazine* and reproduced with his kind permission.

© Ray O'Brien 2005

Published by The Bluecoat Press, Liverpool
Book design by MARCH Graphic Design Studio, Liverpool
Printed by Universities Press, Belfast

ISBN 1 904438-28-8

All rights reserved. No part of this publication may be reproduced, stored in a retrieval system, or transmitted in any form or by any means, electronic, mechanical, photocopying, recording or otherwise, without prior permission from the publisher.

THERE ARE PLACES I'LL REMEMBER

THE BEATLES EARLY VENUES

in and around Merseyside and North Wales

Ray O'Brien

The Bluecoat Press

CONTENTS
VENUES ARE IN LIVERPOOL UNLESS STATED OTHERWISE

INTRODUCTION 8-9

ABATTOIR ATHLETIC AND SOCIAL CLUB 10

AINTREE INSTITUTE 11

AIR TRAINING CORPS CLUB, SOUTHPORT 12

ALBANY CINEMA, MAGHULL 13

ALEXANDRA HALL, CROSBY 14

ALLERTON SYNAGOGUE 15

APOLLO ROLLER RINK, MORETON 16

ASSEMBLY HALL, MOLD 17

BLAIR HALL 18

BUSMENS SOCIAL CLUB (PICTON ROAD) 19

CABARET CLUB 20

CAMBRIDGE HALL, SOUTHPORT 21

CASBAH 22-23

CASSANOVA CLUB (NO 1) 24

CASSANOVA CLUB (NO 2) 25

CAVERN CLUB 26-27

CHILDWALL GOLF CLUB 28

CIVIC HALL, ELLESMERE PORT 29

DAVID LEWIS THEATRE 30

EMBASSY CLUB, WALLASEY 31

EMPIRE THEATRE 32

FLORAL HALL, SOUTHPORT 33

GARSTON BATHS 34

GARSTON STEVEDORES AND DOCKERS CLUB 35

GLEN PARK CLUB, SOUTHPORT 36-37

GRAFTON BALLROOM	38
GREENBANK DRIVE SYNAGOGUE	39
GROSVENOR BALLROOM, WALLASEY	40-41
HAIG HALL CLUB, MORETON	42
HAMBLETON HALL, HUYTON	43
HESWALL JAZZ CLUB, HESWALL	44
HOLYOAKE HALL	45
HULME HALL, PORT SUNLIGHT	46-47
IRBY VILLAGE HALL, IRBY	48-49
IRON DOOR (STORYVILLE JAZZ CLUB)	50
JACARANDA	51
KINGSWAY, SOUTHPORT	52
KNOTTY ASH VILLAGE HALL	53
LA SCALA, RUNCORN	54
LABOUR CLUB, SOUTHPORT	55
LATHOM HALL	56
LEE PARK GOLF CLUB	57
LEWIS'S STORE	58
LITHERLAND TOWN HALL	59
LITTLE THEATRE, SOUTHPORT	60
LIVERPOOL COLLEGE OF ART	61
LOCARNO BALLROOM	62
LOWLANDS	63
MACDONNA HALL, WEST KIRBY	64
MAJESTIC BALLROOM, BIRKENHEAD	65

MERSEYSIDE CIVIL SERVICE CLUB	66
MERSEYVIEW, FRODSHAM	67
MORETON CO-OP HALL, MORETON	68
MORGUE CLUB	69
MOSSWAY HALL	70
MPTE SOCIAL CLUB (FINCH LANE)	71
MV ROYAL IRIS, RIVER MERSEY	72
NEW BRIGHTON PIER, NEW BRIGHTON	73
NEW CABARET ARTISTES CLUB	74
NEW CLUBMOOR HALL	75
NEW COLONY CLUB	76
ODD SPOT CLUB	77
ODEON CINEMA, LLANDUDNO	78-79
ODEON CINEMA	80
ODEON CINEMA, SOUTHPORT	81
PAVILION THEATRE	82-83
PHILLIPS RECORDING STUDIO	84-85
PLAZA BALLROOM, ST HELENS	86
PRESCOT CABLES CLUB, PRESCOT	87
QUARRY BANK HIGH SCHOOL	88
QUEEN'S HALL, WIDNES	89
QUEEN'S HOTEL, SOUTHPORT	90
REGENT BALLROOM, RHYL	91
RIALTO BALLROOM	92
RITZ BALLROOM, RHYL	93
RIVERPARK BALLROOM, CHESTER	94
ROSEBERRY STREET	95

ROYAL LIDO BALLROOM, PRESTATYN 96

ROYALTY THEATRE, CHESTER 97

STARLINE CLUB 98

ST ALOYSIUS YOUTH CLUB, HUYTON 99

ST BARNABUS CHURCH HALL 100

ST EDWARD'S CATHOLIC COLLEGE 101

ST JOHN'S CHURCH HALL 102

ST JOHN'S HALL, BOOTLE 103

ST LUKE'S (JIVE HIVE), CROSBY 104

ST PAUL'S CHURCH HALL, BIRKENHEAD 105

ST PETER'S CHURCH GARDEN FETE 106-107

ST PETER'S CHURCH HALL 108

TECHNICAL COLLEGE, BIRKENHEAD 109

THE INSTITUTE, NESTON 110-111

TOWER BALLROOM, NEW BRIGHTON 112-113

TOWN HALL, EARLSTOWN 114

UPTON GREEN 115

VICTORIA HALL, BEBINGTON 116

WAVERTREE TOWN HALL 117

WILSON HALL 118

WINTER GARDENS 119

WOOLTON VILLAGE CLUB 120

WYVERN SOCIAL CLUB (BLUE ANGEL) 121

YE CRACKE 122

YMCA, BIRKENHEAD 123

YMCA, HOYLAKE 124-125

OTHER VENUES PLAYED 126

THE AUTHOR 127

INTRODUCTION

This book charts the progression of The Beatles' early appearances from their humble origins as The Quarry Men, playing mainly at small venues in South Liverpool, when they performed for little or no recompense, to the larger theatres and ballrooms in the Merseyside area and outlying towns. I have also included North Wales, which has always been a popular destination for Merseysiders, being little more than an hour's drive away. Wherever possible I have obtained photographs of the buildings as they were when the band appeared. I have also included present day pictures, as some of the venues have changed little. Sadly, several have been demolished, with new buildings now standing on the original sites, and some are either car parks, or just waste ground. With each passing year, no doubt, other buildings will follow suit, hence the importance of my photographing them before they change beyond all recognition, or the bulldozer destroys the evidence. Each site, however, whatever has become of it, plays its part in Beatles history.

I have no doubt that The Quarry Men appeared at other venues, especially in their early years between 1957–1959; often at small functions arranged through friends and other contacts which were not recorded. This was before the days of agents and contracts and it was highly unusual for groups to keep a diary record of their appearances. An exception was Harry Prytherch, ex-drummer with The Remo Four and Group One, who noted his band's every engagement and fees paid, and still has the record today. Conversations with Pete Best reveal that the early Beatles often had little idea where they were travelling, especially when in the outer districts of Merseyside, and certainly did not keep a record. It was only after Brian Epstein became their manager that a precise chronicle of their engagements was recorded. Each venue in this book has been carefully researched to authenticate the band's appearance and some have been omitted due to a lack of authenticity. Several people are convinced that The Beatles played at the Orrell Park Ballroom in Liverpool in the early sixties but whilst virtually every other Merseyside band played there, I can find no definite confirmation of a Beatles appearance. The jury must remain out!

Whilst visiting the venues, I was surprised to note how few displayed any reference to The Beatles appearing there. I believe this to be a glaring omission and extremely short-sighted, and would hope that the present owners rectify this and see themselves as a part, albeit a small one, in the history of the greatest band in the world. A notable exception is the Grosvenor Ballroom in Liscard, Wallasey, which boasts a fine plaque on the exterior wall of the building.

I trust that this book will give the reader an insight into The Beatles' early years and the type of venue at which they performed, in common with the hundreds of other bands in Liverpool. It is remarkable that, as late as 1962, they were still appearing at small village halls, to audiences of a hundred or so, Irby Village Hall being a typical example.

Without these early gigs there would have been no Beatles and I will leave the last word to John Lennon who, in 1964 in the USA, said, "It was like going through the eye of a hurricane. One minute we were playing the small clubs in Liverpool, the next we are here!"

Ray O'Brien

ABATTOIR ATHLETIC AND SOCIAL CLUB
PRESCOT ROAD, LIVERPOOL 13

The largest meat market in Britain had a social club attached to the massive premises, which catered for the staff, their families and friends. The Quarry Men appeared here on 16 November 1957, playing either side of the interval, but were not well received and were not rebooked. They had apparently spent some time in the nearby Cattle Market public house and one or two band members were a little the worse for wear! This was an area of the city somewhat unfamiliar to the band, although, as The Beatles, they would go on to make several appearances at St John's Hall in Tuebrook, a little over a mile away.

AINTREE INSTITUTE
1 LONGMOOR LANE, WALTON, LIVERPOOL 9

The Beatles made a total of 31 appearances at this impressive red brick building, all but one of them in 1961. They were promoted by Brian Kelly, who cleverly advertised the venue as, 'Not far from the famous Aintree racecourse – the home of the Grand National'. They made their debut on 7 January, prior to an engagement at Lathom Hall, a distance of approximately three miles from the Institute. Their final engagement at the Institute was on 27 January 1962, by which time Brian Epstein was their manager, and it ended in a degree of acrimony. Kelly paid the band their £15 fee in loose change, which enraged Brian who remarked, "I am having no artists of mine being treated in such a demeaning manner," and he vowed that they would never play at the venue again. Epstein, ever the professional, was at this stage insisting on the group behaving and dressing professionally on stage and, in return, he expected them to be treated as professionals. Later in 1962, the building was sold to a local Catholic church and it became a church social club. Occasional Merseybeat reunions take place at the premises. Brian Epstein is buried in the Jewish cemetery at nearby Long Lane in section A, grave H12.

AIR TRAINING CORPS CLUB
UPPER AUGHTON ROAD, BIRKDALE, SOUTHPORT

The Beatles made just one appearance at this somewhat out of the way venue on 9 March 1961, the first of two appearances that evening in Southport. They were paid £10 between them before travelling the three miles or so to fulfil their second engagement at the High Park Labour Club. The resort town of Southport was a popular location for the band in the early 1960s and they appeared at no fewer than nine different venues at this attractive holiday destination, which is approximately twenty miles from Liverpool.

ALBANY CINEMA
NORTHWAY, MAGHULL, LIVERPOOL 31

Opened on 28 September 1955 with 1,400 seats, it was converted into two cinemas and a bingo hall in 1975 and re-named the Astra. It closed on 6 May 1995, the last films shown being, 'The Shawshank Redemption' and 'Little Women'. A supermarket currently occupies the site. The Beatles made one appearance here on 15 October 1961 at a Sunday afternoon charity concert organised by Jim Gretty who, whilst working at Hessy's music store, sold John Lennon his first guitar. The beneficiaries were the local St John's Ambulance Brigade. Topping the bill was comedian Ken Dodd who is reported to have been unimpressed with The Beatles' music and complained to the organiser! The Beatles did a ten minute spot as part of the three hour, sixteen act bill.

ALEXANDRA HALL
COLLEGE ROAD, CROSBY, LIVERPOOL 23

The Beatles made one appearance here on 19 January 1961 in a show promoted by Brian Kelly. Apart from Alexandra Hall, Kelly also ran promotions at Aintree Institute, Lathom Hall and Litherland Town Hall under the name of Beekay Promotions. The building was opened in 1888 and was originally called Alexandra Assembly Hall and known locally as Rodways Room. In 1902 it became Crosby Town Hall and was used as a Magistrates Court until it closed in the early 1990s. It was demolished in 2004 and a luxury apartment development will occupy the site – appropriately called Alexandra Court.

ALLERTON SYNAGOGUE
BOOKER AVENUE, LIVERPOOL 18

The Beatles appeared here at a Sunday afternoon dance in the hall adjacent to the synagogue. Whilst no actual date has been recorded, it was shortly after Brian Epstein became their manager and those who attended the dance recollect it as sometime in December 1961. Epstein may have been responsible for a previous booking at Greenbank Drive Synagogue which his family attended and undoubtedly used his connections with the Jewish community to secure this engagement. At this time, Paul was living just a mile away in Forthlin Road and, in his teenage years, he would often cycle or walk to John's home in Woolton through the nearby Allerton golf course.

APOLLO ROLLER RINK
195 PASTURE ROAD, MORETON, WIRRAL

In the early 1960s, Tony Booth and Derek Holmes, local promoters, persuaded the rink's owner Mrs Sarah Oburn, known locally as Ma Oburn, to allow Rock and Twist Nights to take place on Monday evenings. Cadbury's factory situated nearby had recently opened and the Rock nights proved very popular with the girls that were employed there. Many Mersey bands appeared at the Apollo, including The Beatles on 26 March 1962. They were paid £20 and admission, which was pay-on-the-door, was four shillings. Ma Oburn was a formidable character, who was not averse to striking customers or group members with her walking stick if they upset her! The band's association with Moreton included an appearance at the Co-operative Hall and, as The Quarry Men, an engagement at the Haig Club in nearby Haig Avenue. The Apollo is still flourishing as a dance club and is little changed, although Mrs Oburn's house, which was adjacent to the premises, has long been demolished.

ASSEMBLY HALL
HIGH STREET, MOLD, NORTH WALES

The Beatles made one appearance here on 24 January 1963. They were paid £50 – an extremely large fee, as other bands who appeared at the venue, including The Searchers, received, on average, just £8. The local council had at first been very reluctant to pay them any more than the other groups and spent a considerable time in discussion before ratifying the deal. They had been booked for two hours and spent the early evening in a nearby hostelry, The Crosskeys, and were a little the worse for wear on arrival. This, however, does not appear to have affected their performance and the council agreed it had been money well spent. Ironically, the hall did not sell alcohol, which may explain the boys' earlier exploits! The building has little changed and is now a bank situated right in the centre of this bustling market town, not far from the border with England. Before setting off for this engagement, the band had made a personal appearance at NEMS record store in Whitechapel, Liverpool, signing copies of their new single, 'Please Please Me'.

BLAIR HALL
162 WALTON ROAD, LIVERPOOL 4

Another of the venues that was part of the Liverpool Co-operative Society, The Beatles appeared here on five occasions, all in 1961. It was used as a jive hive by Peak Promotions, who also organised weekly dances at Holyoake Hall in Wavertree, the David Lewis Theatre in Great George Place and Columba Hall in Widnes. The Beatles first played at Blair Hall on 5 February 1961, with Pete Best experiencing problems with his drum kit. Blair Hall had a sloping stage and he could not prevent his bass drum from moving forwards. Harry Prytherch, drummer with The Remo Four, was familiar with the stage and came to Pete's rescue by tying some string around the drum and his seat! All the other Beatles' engagements at Blair Hall took place in July that year. Long demolished, a supermarket now occupies the site.

BUSMENS SOCIAL CLUB
PICTON ROAD, WAVERTREE, LIVERPOOL 15

Harry Harrison, George's father, was a bus driver and, for a time, secretary of the social committee. Whenever the opportunity arose, he would use his influence to obtain bookings for George and The Quarry Men. Early in 1959 they appeared at the club in Finch Lane and also at Picton Road, less than a mile away from George's birthplace at 12 Arnold Grove. With his wife he also ran ballroom dancing classes at the Speke social club for ten years. Surprisingly there is no record of the band playing there, although it must be a possibility. Of all The Beatles, George's family were probably the most supportive, although Jim McCartney offered Paul every encouragement. As well as George's father getting bookings for them in the early days, his mother would allow the band to rehearse in her home and, when they became famous, spent hours replying personally to fan mail sent to George. Sadly, she died in 1970 predeceasing her husband by eight years.

CABARET CLUB
28 DUKE STREET, LIVERPOOL 1

Brian Epstein had been anxious to introduce The Beatles to the cabaret circuit but this booking proved to be an unmitigated disaster. The club, which Brian frequented socially, catered for a quieter, more sophisticated clientele who preferred music by the likes of Tony Bennett, so when The Beatles opened with 'Money' it did not go down too well! Their one and only appearance at the club, for which they received a £15 fee, was on 25 July 1962 and, needless to say, they were not rebooked. Situated a little further up Duke Street was the Zodiac Coffee Club, a venue much frequented by The Beatles and other local bands. On one famous occasion, The Beatles had a lengthy jam session with The Big Three, Rory Storm and The Hurricanes and Gerry and The Pacemakers. Cilla Black used to work behind the counter and it was at the Zodiac that she met her future husband. The Cabaret Club stood on the corner of Campbell Street and Duke Street. The building was demolished recently and replaced by a modern office block.

CAMBRIDGE HALL
LORD STREET, SOUTHPORT

The Beatles made one appearance here on 26 July 1962, the first of two consecutive engagements, promoted by Brian Epstein's NEMS Enterprises organisation, the second being the following evening at the Tower Ballroom in New Brighton. Joe Brown, whose recording of 'A Picture of You' was number three in the charts at the time, topped a bill which also included Gerry and the Pacemakers, The Big Three, The 4 Jays and Pete McLaine and the Dakotas. Joe Brown had shot to fame following appearances on the popular TV programme of the time 'Six Five Special'. 'A Picture of You' was also used by The Beatles in their stage act and sung by George Harrison. Cambridge Hall is now the Southport Arts Centre and stages a diverse variety of events and concerts.

CASBAH COFFEE CLUB
8 HAYMANS GREEN, WEST DERBY, LIVERPOOL 12

Situated in the cellar of a large Victorian house owned by Peter's mother, Mrs Mona Best, the Casbah was opened on 29 August 1959. Mrs Best had watched a London-based TV pop programme in 1959 and had decided that Liverpool required a venue to match the coffee bar clubs in the capital which were very popular at this time. Mona was aware that there was a mass market of teenage musicians in Liverpool who had nowhere to play and set about recruiting a resident band and The Quarry Men were enlisted. The four-man line-up on the opening night was John Lennon, Paul McCartney, George Harrison and Ken Brown. This line-up appeared at the club on a further six occasions without a drummer, before a dispute over money saw Brown leave the band and team up with Pete Best in a group called The Black Jacks. It would be almost a year before John, Paul and George returned to the club and invited Pete to join them as their drummer. Their first engagement on return from their first trip to Hamburg was not Litherland Town Hall, as is often stated, but the Casbah on 17 December 1960. The band, in their various guises, played at the Casbah on at least 44 occasions and there were possibly more unrecorded appearances. Closed on 24 June 1962, it was reopened in June 2002 as a tourist attraction and still includes the bar ceiling signed by all four original Beatles and a painting of John Lennon by his first wife Cynthia above the fireplace.

CASSANOVA CLUB (1)
DALE STREET, LIVERPOOL 2

The original Cassanova Club was situated above the Temple Restaurant at 24 Dale Street, which was a popular eating establishment for the city's office workers. The club was launched on Sunday 10 January 1960 by the popular local band Cass and the Cassanovas and The Beatles played a ten minute afternoon spot. The Cassanovas were named after their leader, Brian Casser, thus the misspelling of Casanova! The club was only active for a short period and Sam Leach, who had taken over the venue, moved it to larger premises above Sampson and Barlows in London Road. The Beatles would appear at this venue on seven occasions.

CASSANOVA CLUB
39 LONDON ROAD, LIVERPOOL 3

The Cassanova Club had moved to these premises – part of Sampson and Barlow's Restaurant – on 9 February 1961 from its previous brief location in Dale Street, and was the brainchild of local promoter Sam Leach. Two days later, The Beatles made the first of seven appearances at the club, all of which took place in February and March of that year. Their debut at the club was the first of many they were to undertake for Sam Leach. Their second appearance, on February 14, Valentine's night, also featured four other groups including Rory Storm and the Hurricanes and The Big Three. The club was shut down by the police due to excessive noise but was reopened by Sam Leach, in March 1963, who renamed it the Peppermint Lounge, after the famous New York club of a similar name. In between this period, it had functioned as a night club known as the New Compton. Long demolished, it was situated almost directly opposite the Odeon Cinema.

THE CAVERN CLUB
10 MATHEW STREET, LIVERPOOL 2

The Cavern opened on 16 January 1957 as a jazz club by the Earl of Wharncliffe and was named after Le Caveau Francais Jazz Club. Mathew Street was then a hive of activity with lorryloads of fruit and vegetables being unloaded throughout the day. Fruit importers, fish merchants etc dominated the street, with the Cavern situated next door to a washing machine manufacturer. Books have been written ad nauseam about the club and space does not permit me to write a definitive history of it here, merely to provide some basic details. Alan Sytner, who had been running jazz sessions at the Temple restaurant, needed larger premises to accommodate the growing number of jazz bands and the basement of 10 Mathew Street was empty. It had three alleys and one was used for cloakrooms and admission staff, one for a small stage and where people could listen to the music and the third for dancing. Such was its popularity that, by 1959, membership had reached 25,000 at a venue that could only hold 1,000 at a considerable squeeze. Jazz held sway throughout the late fifties and the first official all beat night was held on 25 May 1960, with Rory Storm and the Hurricanes and Cass and the Cassanovas sharing the bill. The Beatles played here on at least 292 occasions, their first recorded appearance being 9 February 1961 and their final one on 3 August 1963. The Quarry Men had played at the club on 7 August 1957 without Paul, who was at a scout camp, and on 24 January 1958. From all accounts, they were not particularly well received, it still being a bastion of jazz. The Cavern closed on 27 March 1973 following an emotional farewell concert which commenced at 8pm and finished at 3am and the bulldozers moved in shortly after its closure. The new Cavern opened in 1984, constructed on the same side of the road and within yards of the old club. Over 15,000 bricks from the old cellar were used in its reconstruction and it bears a reasonable resemblance to the old one, despite being much cleaner and lacking the unique smell of the original!

CHILDWALL GOLF CLUB
NAYLORS ROAD, LIVERPOOL 25

An early Quarry Men booking arranged by Nigel Whalley and Alan Sytner (see Lee Park) in the summer of 1957. At this time, it was a typical venue for the band who were grateful for any type of booking they could get. They also appeared at Childwall Labour Club and at private functions in the area. It was a part of the city with which they were all familiar, particularly John, who would often frequent the nearby Childwall Abbey public house and other local hostelries.

CIVIC HALL
WHITBY ROAD, ELLESMERE PORT, CHESHIRE

The Beatles' only engagement in this industrial town – home of Vauxhall Motors, approximately 17 miles south of Liverpool – took place on 14 January 1963. The dance was organised by the Wolverham Welfare Association and attracted an audience of seven hundred. Following a rare day off, two days later the band travelled to Manchester for a live appearance on the Granada Television programme 'People and Places'. They then proceeded to the nearby Playhouse Theatre to record some numbers for the BBC radio programme 'Here We Go'. The Civic Hall is still in regular use.

DAVID LEWIS THEATRE
GREAT GEORGE PLACE, LIVERPOOL 1

On 17 October 1961, the newly formed unofficial Beatles fan club hired a room for £5 at the theatre and The Beatles agreed to attend. They had no PA equipment but Paul and Pete Best each sang a couple of numbers, much to the delight of the hundred or so present, who included Paul's father. The fan club was only in existence for a month and the first official club was formed in 1962 by Bobbie Brown from Wallasey, who in turn handed the reins to Frieda Kelly, who ran it until it was officially wound up in 1975. The David Lewis, an imposing building, was situated close to Liverpool's Anglican Cathedral and housed a hotel as well as a theatre. It was demolished in the 1980s as part of road improvements.

EMBASSY CLUB
140 BOROUGH ROAD, WALLASEY, WIRRAL

The Silver Beetles made one appearance at this former cinema in July 1960 and Bob Evans remembers the occasion well. "They had no drummer and took ages setting up their equipment and tuning their guitars, and the audience became very restless." Drummer Tommy Moore had made his final appearance with the band on 13 June that year and Pete Best did not join until August. Borough Road is a short distance from 90 Buchanan Road where Roberta Brown lived and who launched the first official Beatles fan club in May 1962. A short-lived unofficial club had been formed the previous year. Bobby, as she was known, assisted by friends, ran the club until early 1963 when she handed over the responsibility to her friend Frieda Kelly. During her tenure Bobby organised two coach trips to see The Beatles play in Manchester and St Helens. The Embassy is known today as the Embassy Bingo and Social Club. Two miles away, at 268 Wallasey Village, was Albert Marrion Photographers and it was at his premises, on 17 December 1961, that the first publicity photographs of the band were taken.

EMPIRE THEATRE
LIME STREET, LIVERPOOL 1

The Beatles' first appearance at Liverpool's largest theatre was on 28 October 1962, when they were part of a NEMS presentation bill headed by Little Richard. Although they had appeared at the Empire as The Quarry Men in the late fifties in talent contests, this was undoubtedly their most influential booking to date. As The Beatles, they made eight appearances at the Empire. Their most significant appearance was on 7 December 1963, when they taped a special edition for 'Juke Box Jury' which, when screened later that evening, was watched by 23 million viewers. They then did a 45 minute spot, which was also broadcast by the BBC later that evening for a separate show, 'It's The Beatles'. Their final appearance at the Empire was on 5 December 1965, when 40,000 applications were received for the two houses, at a venue with a seating capacity of only 2,500!

FLORAL HALL
THE PROMENADE, SOUTHPORT

The Beatles made four appearances at this popular theatre and it was possibly their most prestigious booking at that stage of their career when they made their debut here on 20 February 1962. John Lennon described it as a, "proper theatre with gold curtains". Four other bands shared the bill including Gerry and the Pacemakers, Rory Storm and the Hurricanes and The Chris Hamilton Jazzmen. The show was advertised as a 'Rock 'n' Trad Spectacular'. Their final appearance took place on 15 October 1963. A modern building has replaced the old theatre and it remains the town's major entertainment venue and attracts local, national and international stars all year round.

GARSTON BATHS
SPEKE ROAD, LIVERPOOL 19

Known locally as The Blood Baths, due to its fearsome reputation, as rival gangs would often meet to do battle there. After dark, the pool area was boarded over and dances were held. The Quarry Men appeared here on several occasions in the late fifties. Colin Hanton attended school in Garston and was probably responsible for the bookings. They also appeared at nearby Wilson Hall and at the Winter Gardens in Heald Street. It has been said that George, who only lived a short bus ride away, would swim at the baths on Saturday mornings. The building was next to the Corporation transport offices and, as well as having a swimming pool, housed a wash house and assembly rooms. The baths were closed some years ago and were finally demolished in 2003.

GARSTON STEVEDORES AND DOCKERS CLUB
73 WINDOW LANE, LIVERPOOL 19

Known locally as the Blue Union Club, The Quarry Men played here in June 1958, not long after George Harrison joined the line-up. It was one of the few appearances that John Lowe made with the band. John Lowe was a pupil at the Liverpool Institute with Paul and George and he and Paul auditioned for the Liverpool Cathedral choir which they both failed! Lowe – nicknamed Duff – had joined the band as a pianist early in 1958 and recorded with them at Percy Phillips studio in Kensington on 12 July 1958. He left the band in January 1959 and joined a country and western group. The original Blue Union was demolished in the 1960s and a new club now stands on the site.

GLEN PARK CLUB
273 LORD STREET, SOUTHPORT

The Beatles made just one appearance at this small club in November1961. Situated directly opposite the Southport Arts Centre (Cambridge Hall), the entrance to the club was situated on a small alleyway off Lord Street with a book shop and a shoe shop now on each corner. The club was ostensibly for the town's middle-class teenagers and was run by Matt Smith. Rory Storm and the Hurricanes also appeared here. Southport is rich in Beatles history and they appeared at no less than nine different venues and possibly ten if one includes an alleged appearance at the town's Palace Hotel. Ron Watson is convinced he saw them there. "I know that The Beatles played at the Palace Hotel one Saturday evening in the Autumn of 1962 because I was there, but I did not make a diary entry of it at the time." Unfortunately, try as I may, I have found nobody to corroborate this account so, as they say, the jury must remain out. The Palace Hotel in its heyday had more than 1,000 rooms and many top stars stayed there including, it is rumoured, Clark Gable and Frank Sinatra. It was demolished in 1969 as, by then, it was suffering from a serious lack of guests. It spanned the land between the Fisherman's Rest on Weld Road, Westcliffe Road, Oxford Road and Palace Road.

LORD STREET, SOUTHPORT.

GRAFTON BALLROOM
WEST DERBY ROAD, LIVERPOOL 6

The first of four appearances by The Beatles at this popular venue took place on 3 August 1962, although as The Quarry Men they had performed here on several occasions in skiffle contests in the late fifties. Opened on 9 February 1924, the Liverpool Echo headline proclaimed, 'Liverpool's biggest dance hall opens. A real Palais de Danse for Merseyside.' On the 12 June 1963 they gave their services for free in aid of a charity concert for the NSPCC. A certain Jeffrey Archer was involved in the fund-raising, having had some involvement in organising the event. In 1965, dance hall scenes for the film, 'Ferry Across the Mersey' starring Gerry and The Pacemakers, were shot at the Grafton. Situated next door to the Locarno, both ballrooms were part of the Mecca organisation, the Grafton remains a very popular dance venue, particularly at the weekends.

GREENBANK DRIVE SYNAGOGUE
MAX MORRIS HALL, GREENBANK DRIVE, LIVERPOOL 17

The Liverpool Jewish community have always provided excellent facilities for their young members and the 1960s were no exception. The Max Morris Hall was a popular venue for local bands, including Derry and The Seniors and the Remo Quartet. During the summer of 1961, The Beatles played here at a fund raising event with tickets priced at five shillings. Brian Epstein's father was an active member of the synagogue and it may have been his influence that initiated the booking. This was around the time that Bill Harry, the editor of Mersey Beat, approached Brian asking him to stock copies of the paper, which had many features concerning The Beatles, thereby nailing the myth that Epstein had no prior knowledge of them until a fan requested one of their recordings at his NEMS Whitechapel store later that year! The synagogue is still flourishing today and has barely changed. It is situated near to the Smithdown Road entrance to Sefton Park.

GROSVENOR BALLROOM
66 GROSVENOR STREET, LISCARD, WALLASEY, WIRRAL

Les Dodd, a local dance promoter, had been promoting dances through his company Paramount Enterprises, Wallasey, at the Grosvenor since 1936. He had a similar arrangement at the Institute in Neston. He had strict rules for his dances and advertised, 'No Rock and Roll,' 'No Jiving' and 'No Teenagers!' However, he reluctantly bowed to the inevitable and commenced booking beat groups at both venues, and The Silver Beetles were the first group he booked at the Institute on 2 June 1960. Two days later, they first appeared at the Grosvenor and they would make a total of fourteen appearances which included three as The Silver Beetles, seven as The Silver Beatles, all in 1960, and four in 1961 as The Beatles. Dodd liaised with Allan Williams who, at this time, was acting as an agent for several local bands, including The Silver Beetles. Their third appearance, on 11 June 1960, was not without incident. They arrived at the Grosvenor without a drummer, as their then drummer Tommy Moore's girlfriend had, in no uncertain terms, told him to quit the band. John Lennon jokingly invited anyone from the audience who could play the drums to join them on stage. He was somewhat taken aback when the local teenage gang leader Ronnie, from all accounts a fearsome character, stepped up and it soon became apparent that he had no idea how to play at all. Despite their pleas, he would not leave the stage and insisted on playing with them. It was only the intervention of Allan Williams, who having arrived at the interval, used his powers of verbal persuasion to remove Ronnie from the stage! The Grosvenor today is little changed externally and internally, and a plaque on the outside wall serves as a reminder of The Beatles' appearances there.

GROSVENOR Ballroom

TO-NIGHT SATURDAY	SWING SESSION 8.0 to 11-45 "The Beatles"	Adm.3/-
TUESDAY NEXT	PARAMOUNT DANCE 8.0 to 11.30 "21 - Plus Night"	Adm 2/6
COMING SOON	ROCKING SESSION 8.0 to 11-45 "The Remo 4"	Adm 3/-

BOOK THE POPULAR GROSVENOR BALLROOM FOR YOUR NEXT FUNCTION! Full details from Entertainment Manager 142, Brighton Street, Wallasey, (Phone Wall. 1600, Ext. 35)

GROSVENOR BALLROOM, LISCARD
TO - NIGHT (SATURDAY)
SWING SESSION
featuring the Sensational New Group
" THE BEATLES "
8 - 0 to 11 - 45   ADMISSION 3/-

Paramount Enterprises
DANCE AND CONCERT PROMOTION ETC.
TELEPHONE NEW BRIGHTON 1232
67 SEABANK ROAD
WALLASEY CHESHIRE

LWD/VJ

A.R. Williams, Esq.,
23, Slater Street,
LIVERPOOL, 1.

20th May, 1960.

Dear Mr. Williams,

Further to our telephone conversations regarding the alteration of the booking for Whit Monday at the Grosvenor Ballroom, I now have pleasure in enclosing an amended Contract covering the engagement of Gerry & The Pace-Makers and The Silver Beetles.

Will you please sign and return the original Contract, retaining the copy for your files. I should also be obliged if you will return the Contract held by you in respect of Cass & His Cassanovas for Whit Monday.

With best wishes,

Yours sincerely,

HAIG HALL CLUB
HAIG AVENUE, MORETON, WIRRAL

Situated in a cul-de-sac off Sandy Lane, the Haig was a popular local community club which featured many bands from the Merseyside area in the late fifties and early sixties, including Gerry and the Pacemakers. The Quarry Men also appeared here in November 1957, for what was possibly their Wirral debut. The Haig closed for business in the late seventies to the dismay of many, but to the delight of others, who were relieved to be no longer subject to excessive noise, particularly at the weekends. Private houses now stand on the site of the club.

HAMBLETON HALL
ST DAVID'S ROAD, PAGE MOSS, LIVERPOOL 14

Hambleton Hall had a somewhat fearsome reputation, with Paul McCartney recalling evenings ending in fights between rival gangs. The Beatles made 16 appearances here, all but one in 1961, their final engagement occurring on 13 January 1962. Brian Epstein was by now their manager and this was not the type of place at which he wanted groups of his appearing. Billed as the 'Sensational Beatles' they had made their debut on 25 January 1961 on a bill with Faron and the Tempest Tornadoes and Derry and the Seniors. It was here that local promoter Sam Leach saw The Beatles for the first time and was so impressed he decided to book them for his shows. Bob Wooler also promoted shows at this venue, as did many other freelance promoters. The building later became a Probation Office and is now demolished.

HESWALL JAZZ CLUB
BARNSTON WOMEN'S INSTITUTE, BARNSTON ROAD, HESWALL, WIRRAL

The Beatles made the first of three appearances at this somewhat out of the way venue on 24 March 1962, when they wore their smart Beno Dorn suits for the first time. Dorn's business at 5 Grange Road West, Birkenhead, was advertised as, 'The master tailor for impeccable handmade clothes' and Brian Epstein, having decided the band needed to spruce up their image, some days earlier had taken the boys to Dorn to be fitted out. The suits, with matching ties, were priced at £40 each, but Brian, ever the businessman, was able to successfully negotiate a price of £30! Anne Robertson, current President of the Institute, recalls them, "carrying the suits up our path and wearing them for the very first time on our stage!" Back then the hall was let to the Heswall Jazz Club who held a weekly jazz night there. Chris Wharton was responsible for the bookings and doorman Bill Slater remembers The Beatles' appearances well. Their next appearance was on 30 June that year when they shared the bill with The Big Three and their final engagement at the club was on 25 September 1962. In 1964, Paul paid £8,750 for 'Rembrandt', a house in nearby Baskervyle Road for his father Jim and, as a child, Ringo spent six months at the town's children's hospital convalescing from pleurisy.

HOLYOAKE HALL
332–338 SMITHDOWN ROAD, LIVERPOOL 15

Situated on the corners of Blenheim Road and Cramond Avenue, this large impressive red brick building is just a few hundred yards from Penny Lane. It was owned by the Liverpool Co-operative Society. The ballroom was on the first floor and played host to a variety of entertainers, including two appearances by The Beatles in July 1961. The Quarry Men had appeared here in skiffle contests in the late fifties and it was also a popular venue for many other Liverpool bands. It had a reputation for rather heavy-handed doormen in their dealing with the fans of the various groups. Still standing, it has changed little, externally at least, since The Beatles played here.

HULME HALL
BOLTON ROAD, PORT SUNLIGHT, WIRRAL

The first of four appearances by The Beatles at Hulme Hall, all in 1962, took place on 7 July but it was their second and final engagements which were highly significant. Their second appearance, on 18 August, was Ringo Starr's official debut with the band, although he had played with them before in an unofficial capacity. They appeared next on 6 October and finally on 27 October, when, prior to going on stage, they recorded a radio interview for the patients of Cleaver and Clatterbridge Hospitals. The seven minute interview was conducted by Monty Lister and his two young assistants, Peter Smethurst and Malcolm Threadgill. This was The Beatles' first ever radio interview and was broadcast the following day. Brian Epstein arrived at the hall after the interview had been concluded and was apparently not best pleased that he had not been informed. Radio Clatterbridge, located in the grounds of Clatterbridge Hospital, still broadcasts 24 hours a day. Hulme Hall is situated in the delightful and picturesque model village of Port Sunlight, built by Viscount Leverhulme in 1888 to house his factory workers. The hall itself was built in 1901, taking Mrs Lever's maiden name and first used as a women's dining room. During the Second World War it served as a billet for the American troops who dealt with American ammunition ships using the nearby Bromborough Docks.

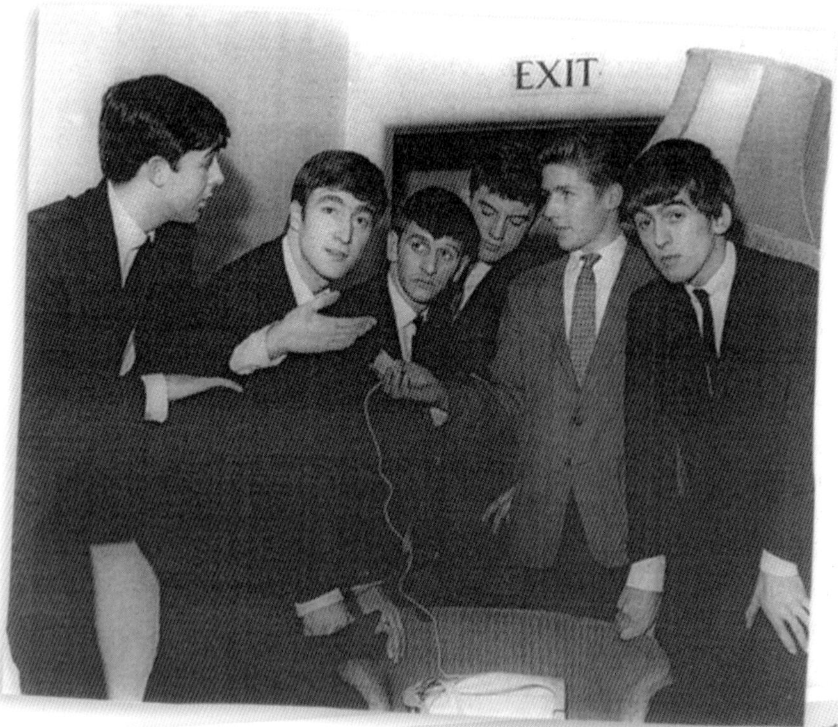
EXIT

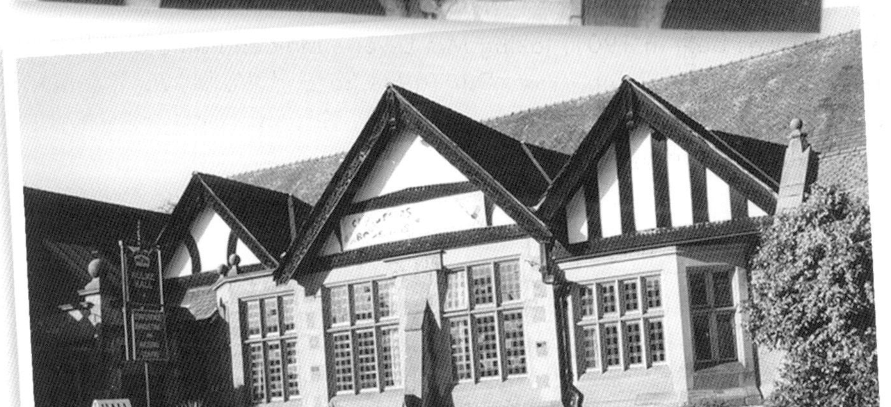
HALL FOR HIRE

IRBY VILLAGE HALL
THINGWALL ROAD, IRBY, WIRRAL

The building was opened on 15 October 1938 as a community centre for the village. During the Second World War, it was used for school purposes for children from Guernsey who had been evacuated to Irby. The Home Guard also used the premises on two evenings a week. Following the cessation of hostilities, the hall staged several amateur dramatic productions as well as various other social activities. The Beatles appeared here on 7 September 1962 for the Newton Dancing School and approximately one hundred people were present. They were contracted to play for one hour for a fee of £35 but the organisers did not have enough money to pay them the full amount on the night, and a jumble sale had to be held the following week at the bowling club opposite, to raise the balance that they were owed! The owner of the dancing school, Mary Newton, organised numerous similar events at the hall and other acts included The Big Three and Freddie Starr and the Midnighters. Numerous fans from all over the world visited the hall in 2002 to mark the 40th anniversary of their only appearance. Externally the hall has altered little since The Beatles' appearance. The main entrance by which they would have entered was situated at the side of the building, a new extension at the front being added in the 1970s. Inside, the room which The Beatles changed in is still there, as is the small bar area, which in those days sold non-alcoholic drinks. The dance floor is regarded as one of the finest in the Wirral and remains much the same, although the original stage they performed on is no longer there. Irby Village Hall lies well back from Thingwall Road, about 100 metres on the Birkenhead side of the village, and is still in active use today, providing a wide variety of activities for the local community.

A DANCE
will be held at the
VILLAGE HALL, IRBY
to be held on
Friday, 7th September 1962
The Beatles and the Courting Group
8-0 p.m. till 11-30 p.m.
—:—
TICKETS—7/6 each

NEMS ENTERPRISES LTD
DIRECTORS: B. AND C. J. EPSTEIN

12-14 WHITECHAPEL, LIVERPOOL, 1   TELEPHONE ROYAL 7895

BE/BA:

30th July 1962

Dear Mrs. Newton,

With further regard to our recent telephone conversation in connection with a booking for THE BEATLES, at the 'Village Hall', at Newton Dancing School, Irby on Friday September 7th. I would now confirm this engagement at a fee of £25 and that playing time will be one hour.

Perhaps you will advise me nearer the date of the exact location of the venue and also at what time you wish the group to be present on that evening.

Yours sincerely,
Brian Epstein.

Mrs. M.A. Newton,
Dawpool Lodge,
Thurstaston.
Wirral

IRON DOOR CLUB
13 TEMPLE STREET, LIVERPOOL 2

The Iron Door, also known as the Storyville Jazz Club, actually had an iron door, the old wooden one having been replaced after an axe-wielding gang had attempted to gain entry whilst pursuing members of one of the bands playing there. If the Cavern was The Beatles' spiritual home, then the Iron Door belonged to that other influential band, The Searchers. In fact, The Beatles made just seven appearances here, four in March 1961 and three in March 1962, the final one on the 15th on a bill advertised as 'The Beatles Farewell Party'. The Iron Door hosted many all night sessions organised by the promoter Sam Leach. On 11 March 1961, approximately 2,000 people crammed into the club which was designed for half that number, for a 12-hour, 12-band session, which commenced at 8pm on the Saturday and finished at 8am the following morning! Now demolished, all that remains of its illustrious past is a carpark.

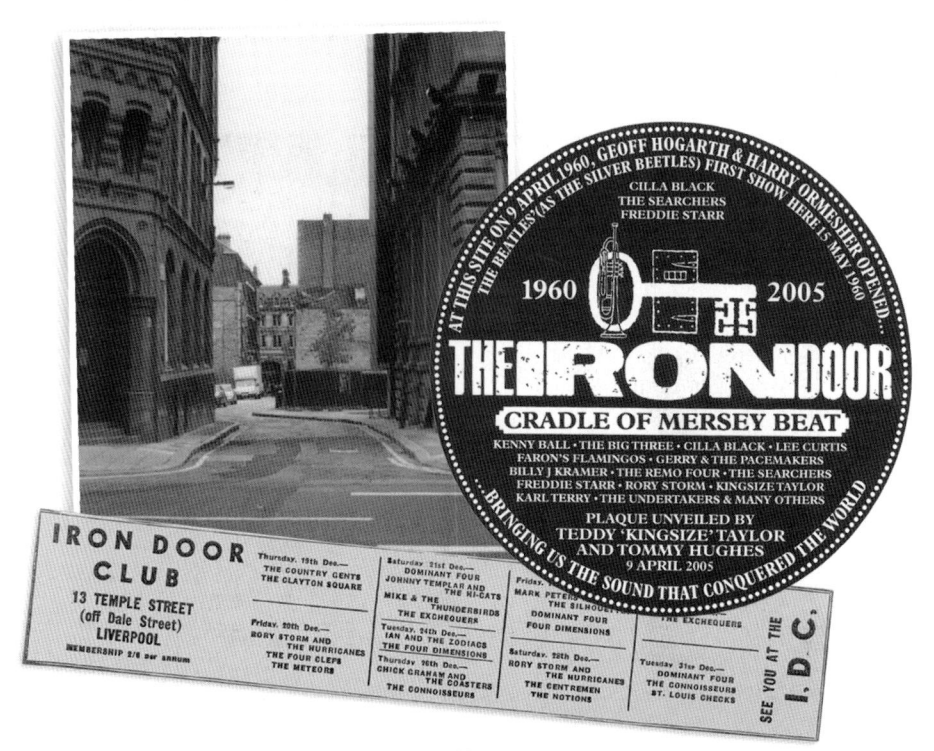

JACARANDA COFFEE BAR
23 SLATER STREET, LIVERPOOL 1

Opened by Allan Williams in September 1958, the Jacaranda was a favourite meeting place for solicitors, doctors, students and musicians, including the young Beatles, Gerry Marsden and Rory Storm. Williams asked Stuart Sutcliffe and a fellow art student Rod Murray to paint some murals in the club. Some writers state that John Lennon also assisted Stuart, but this is yet another Beatles myth! The band first played at the Jacaranda on 30 May 1960, billed as The Silver Beetles. This was also their first engagement since returning from their tour of Scotland with Johnny Gentle. It is impossible to say how many times they played here, as most of their appearances were not documented other than a further appearance on 13 June that year. This was drummer Tommy Moore's final appearance with the band. It has been estimated that they probably made a dozen appearances in all. In later years it changed its name but, in the early eighties, it reopened as the Jacaranda. A popular tourist haunt, it has changed much from the days when The Beatles played here, having expanded and now bearing little resemblance to Allan Williams' original club.

KINGSWAY CLUB
THE PROMENADE, SOUTHPORT

When Brian Epstein became The Beatles' manager he immediately set about developing their professional image, for instance persuading them to wear suits on stage. He also insisted that they would, whilst honouring existing bookings, no longer play at the more seedy dance halls in which they had usually appeared at the start of the sixties. Their debut at the Kingsway, on 22 January 1962, was a good example of this policy, as this venue had carpets and possessed a real stage with curtains! They would play here a total of eight times, all in 1962, their final appearance taking place on 23 July. On their second appearance on 29 January, Pete Best was ill and a certain Ringo Starr, then with Rory Storm and the Hurricanes, replaced him on drums. The building is currently up for sale and most recently has functioned as a night club named Bliss.

KNOTTY ASH VILLAGE HALL
EAST PRESCOT ROAD, LIVERPOOL 14

The first of eight appearances at this impressive building took place on 15 September 1961, promoted by Mona Best. She was responsible for their first seven bookings at this venue, when she acted in her capacity as unofficial manager to the band. Their final appearance was promoted by Sam Leach, Mrs Best having declined her option on the booking. The event was a 'St Patrick's Night Rock Gala' and took place on 17 March 1962. They shared a bill with Rory Storm and the Hurricanes which was arranged by Leach to help pay for his engagement party, which took place in nearby Huyton immediately after the show, and which lasted until the following afternoon! Both bands attended the party, as did Brian Epstein. Knotty Ash Village Hall is little changed and is situated almost opposite Thomas Lane, home to Liverpool's favourite comedian Ken Dodd.

LA SCALA, HIGH STREET
RUNCORN, CHESHIRE

The Beatles made two appearances at this venue, approximately six miles from Liverpool Airport. The first, on 16 October 1962, was the evening before their first ever live performance on TV for a local programme called 'People and Places', when they sang two numbers, 'Love Me Do' and 'Some Other Guy'. Ironically, this predated their first live Radio interview by ten days when they were interviewed at Hulme Hall Port Sunlight, by Monty Lister and his two young assistants Peter Smethurst and Malcolm Threadgill for hospital radio. In that interview, Paul McCartney revealed that he felt more nervous than at their TV debut. Their final appearance at La Scala was on 11 December 1962, one week before their fifth and final trip to Hamburg. Originally opened as a cinema, La Scala was a dance hall until the 1970s, and is now a bingo hall. The building remains much the same and is now known as simply The Scala.

LABOUR CLUB
DEVONSHIRE ROAD, HIGH PARK, SOUTHPORT

The Beatles made one appearance here in March 1961, having played at the ATC club in Birkdale earlier that evening. At this time, clubs such as this were extremely popular and to a certain extent still are today. There were over 300 in Merseyside alone affiliated to the Merseyside Clubs Association. They generally featured country and western type singers, comedians, and cabaret style entertainers. Beat groups would be booked occasionally and most of the Liverpool bands performed at this type of venue. The club is still active and is now called the Devonshire.

LATHOM HALL
LATHOM AVENUE, SEAFORTH, LIVERPOOL 21

Built originally in 1884 as a cinema, it became a venue for local promoter Brian Kelly as well as Litherland Town Hall and the Aintree Institute. He would audition bands who would play for no fee with the promise that if successful he would offer them work. On 14 May 1960, as The Silver Beats, they gave a brief performance on a bill that also included Kingsize Taylor and the Dominoes and impressed Kelly who booked them for an official engagement at Lathom Hall the following week. However, they then embarked on a tour of Scotland with Johnny Gentle without informing Kelly, and so did not appear. Kelly was so annoyed that he did not book them again for several months. The Beatles went on to make a further ten appearances, all in 1961. It was at Lathom Hall that the band got involved in a fight with a local gang of youths, with Stuart Sutclifffe bearing the brunt of the assault and John Lennon, whilst defending him, sustaining a broken finger. It should be added that there is no evidence to suggest Stuart suffered head injuries as a result of this incident which eventually led to his fatal brain haemorrhage, as has been suggested by some writers. Lathom Hall is still active today.

LEE PARK GOLF CLUB
KINGS DRIVE, GATEACRE, LIVERPOOL 25

On leaving school Nigel Whalley, the tea-chest player with The Quarry Men, became an apprentice golf professional at Lee Park. At the club, Nigel also played golf with Dr Sytner, whose son Alan had just opened the Cavern Club, then a jazz venue. Nigel approached Alan about a possible booking for The Quarry Men at the Cavern and Alan said he would like to see them perform at the golf club first. They passed the audition and two weeks later, on 7 August 1957, made their Cavern debut. Alan was also responsible for them obtaining a further booking at Childwall Golf Club. Whilst Nigel's career as a musician was short-lived, he went on to become a successful professional golfer. He maintained contact with John Lennon throughout The Beatles' career, having been a pal of John's from the age of five. Paul and his younger brother Michael attended Joseph Williams Primary School in nearby Naylorsfield Road, where they both passed the scholarship at the age of eleven.

LEWIS'S DEPARTMENT STORE
40 RANELAGH STREET, LIVERPOOL 1

The Beatles made one appearance at Liverpool's famous department store on 28 November 1962 for a 'Young Idea Dance' held on the top floor for members of staff. They were paid £25. The main entrance, situated opposite the Adelphi Hotel, was a popular rendezvous for courting couples, including John and Cynthia. High above the doors is a statue of a naked man created by the sculptor Jacob Epstein which was highly controversial when first erected, although these days is hardly given a second glance! It has been immortalised in the Spinners' song 'In My Liverpool Home' which contains the line, 'We meet under a statue exceedingly bare!' For a short while Paul worked as a driver's assistant on one of the store's delivery vans. Across the road from Lewis's, in Great Charlotte Street, was Blacklers' store, where George served a brief apprenticeship as an electrician.

LITHERLAND TOWN HALL
HATTON HILL ROAD, LIVERPOOL 21

Of the 20 appearances which The Beatles made at this venue, the most significant was their first, on 27 December 1960. They had recently returned from their first trip to Hamburg and the gig was advertised as 'Direct from Hamburg – The Beatles!' Prior to going to Hamburg, they were not particularly well known and many people turned up expecting to see a German band! However, their time in Hamburg had transformed them into a dynamic outfit and they gave an incredible performance. They never really looked back after this night and the bookings flooded in. This was not their first local engagement since their return from Germany, as some writers have suggested, having appeared at the Casbah on the 17 December and the Grosvenor Ballroom in Wallasey on Christmas Eve. Another memorable appearance at Litherland Town Hall occurred on 19 October 1961 when they combined with Gerry and the Pacemakers to give a single, four-number performance as The Beatmakers. Their last appearance was on 9 November 1961, yet another significant date in Beatles' history, for earlier in the day, at the Cavern, a certain Brian Epstein saw them perform for the first time. Litherland Town Hall is currently being refurbished and is re-opening as a £3million medical centre.

THE LITTLE THEATRE
HOGHTON STREET, SOUTHPORT

Whilst undertaking a six-night residency at the Odeon Cinema in Southport from Monday 26 to Saturday 31 August 1963, The Beatles participated in a documentary for the BBC about the Mersey Beat boom. Part of the filming was meant to be live footage from a concert at the Odeon but had to be aborted due to sound difficulties, caused by the hysterical reaction of the audience. An alternative venue was sought and filming commenced at the nearby Little Theatre on Tuesday 27 August at 10am. Assistant floor manager Charles Preston remembers the occasion well. "The Beatles changed into their collarless suits whilst their equipment was set up and, as John Lennon had a sore throat, I was sent to Boots for pastilles before work could start! Filming finished at 5.30pm and Ringo admired the theatre so much that he even enquired about becoming a member!" The film was then cut and dubbed with audience reaction from the previous evening's show at the Odeon and was broadcast on Wednesday 9 October entitled, 'The Mersey Sound'. The documentary also featured two other local bands – Group One and the Undertakers. The Little Theatre is still flourishing and presents some excellent productions.

LIVERPOOL COLLEGE OF ART
HOPE STREET, LIVERPOOL 1

John Lennon was a student here from 1957 to 1960. It was at the college that he met his first wife Cynthia and became close friends with Stuart Sutcliffe and Bill Harry, who went on to become the editor of the Mersey Beat newspaper. Paul McCartney and George Harrison were pupils at the Liverpool Institute High School next door and they and John and Stuart would rehearse at lunchtimes in the Art College's 'life room', which was situated on the top floor of the building. As a band they played quite regularly at the Saturday evening Student Union dances in the early months of 1960. They used the college's amplifier, being without one themselves, with the proviso that it was not removed from the premises. However, they disregarded this rule and allegedly took it with them to Hamburg, forgetting to bring it home with them! I have also heard that John sold it in Hamburg to raise money for food but I would take this story with a large pinch of salt! A great influence on John at the college was teacher Arthur Ballard, who perhaps saw in John something of himself. Ballard was a tough, no-nonsense man with an off-beat sense of humour, who, whilst recognising that John's artistic abilities were limited compared to Stuart's, offered him every encouragement. John never returned to the college following The Silver Beetles' tour of Scotland with Johnny Gentle. He briefly shared a flat at nearby 3 Gambier Terrace with Stuart Sutcliffe and another student from the college, Rod Murray.

LOCARNO BALLROOM
WEST DERBY ROAD, LIVERPOOL 6

Opened on Easter Monday 1905 as the Olympia Theatre seating 3,750, it converted to a cinema in March 1925 and closed in 1939, when it was used as a storage depot during the Second World War. In 1949, it re-opened as a ballroom named the Locarno, and The Beatles made one appearance on 14 February 1963 at a special dance to celebrate St Valentine's Day. Tickets cost 3^s 6^d (17.5 pence) – an amazingly low amount when one considers that they had already had two national chart successes. The Quarry Men had appeared here in the late fifties at skiffle contests. The ballroom closed in 1964 and became a bingo hall, with the late Bob Wooler acting as a bingo caller in the seventies. It has now returned to its former name and hosts a variety of concerts.

LOWLANDS, WEST DERBY COMMUNITY ASSOCIATION
HAYMANS GREEN, LIVERPOOL 12

The Quarry Men took part in a Saturday night audition in June 1958. They were unsuccessful and obtained no further bookings. However, when The Quarry Men briefly stopped performing at the end of 1958, George Harrison joined The Les Stewart Quartet and appeared several times with them early in 1959 at Lowlands. Fifty metres away, on the opposite side of the road, was Pete Best's home, which was to become the Casbah, officially opening on 29 August 1959, and where The Beatles would appear on numerous occasions. Lowlands still plays an active role in the community and the Casbah reopened in 2002 with Pete Best and his band performing there occasionally. Lowlands is somewhat surprisingly overlooked by fans visiting the Casbah, despite its close proximity.

WEST DERBY COMMUNITY ASSOCIATION
"READY TO SERVE TOGETHER"
"LOWLANDS", HAYMANS GREEN, WEST DERBY, LIVERPOOL L12 7JG
Telephone: 0151 226 5352
REGISTERED CHARITY No. 507 240

MACDONNA HALL (THISTLE CAFE)
34 BANKS ROAD, WEST KIRBY, WIRRAL

This was the first engagement from which Brian Epstein took a commission from the band's fee. They were paid £18, Brian receiving 10 per cent. The Beatles appeared here only once, on 1 February 1962, with the event promoted as the 'Grand Opening Of The Beatle Club', which was down to Epstein's powers of persuasion more than anything else. Promoter Sam Leach maintains that Rory Storm stood in for John Lennon who was ill. Whilst this is possible, it remains unsubstantiated, although it is not disputed that John did not appear that evening. At the time, the ground floor of the building was an eating area called the Thistle Café, with a dance studio where The Beatles played situated directly above. A hairdressers now occupies the first floor, with a restaurant below. The late Derek Taylor, who acted as The Beatles' Press Officer, worked initially as a journalist for the Hoylake and West Kirby Advertiser.

MAJESTIC BALLROOM
46 CONWAY STREET, BIRKENHEAD, WIRRAL

The Beatles made a total of 17 appearances at this venue, which was owned by the massive Top Rank entertainment organisation. Their debut, on 28 June 1962, was their first ever booking with Top Rank, who owned 28 ballrooms in Britain, the majority called the Majestic. On 17 August 1962, their stand-in drummer was Johnny Hutchison of The Big Three, Pete Best having left the band the previous day, and his replacement, Ringo Starr, being still contracted to Rory Storm and the Hurricanes. Johnny Hutchison was regarded by many as Liverpool's finest drummer. Ringo would make his debut the following evening at Hulme Hall in nearby Port Sunlight. By the time, The Beatles appeared at the Majestic on 17 January 1963, every ticket was sold out, with five hundred angry fans outside unable to get in. Consequently, two further shows were arranged for 31 January and 21 February, when they played to two separate houses on each night at 8pm and 11pm, a most unusual occurrence for a ballroom back then. Their final appearance was on 10 April 1963. The building lay derelict for a number of years but, at the time of writing, is a somewhat upmarket Chinese Restaurant.

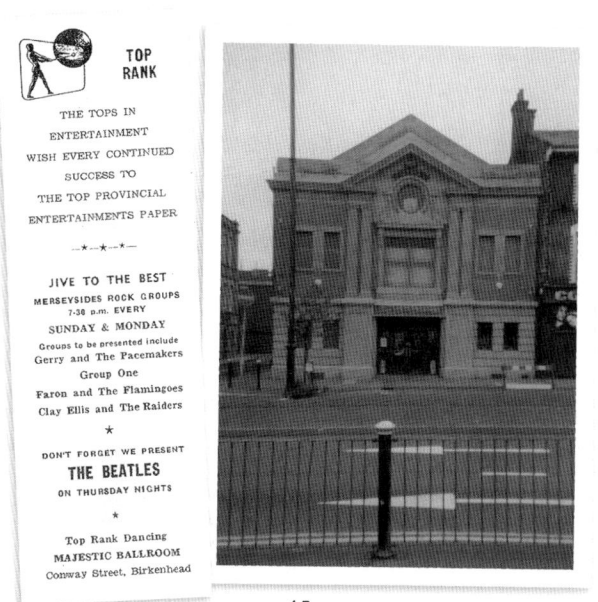

MERSEYSIDE CIVIL SERVICE CLUB
LOWER CASTLE STREET, LIVERPOOL 2

The Beatles made four appearances here, all in November 1961, and Maurice Daniels former drummer with Alby and the Sorrals, remembers the occasions well. "I attended all four sessions, which I suppose was only fair as I had been pushing the secretary to book them! They were paid £15 and, surprisingly, the gigs were not that well supported and, in view of their fee being much higher than most bands at that time, they were given no more bookings." The club was relinquished by the Civil Service Sports Society in the early seventies and in more recent times has been known as the Castle Court.

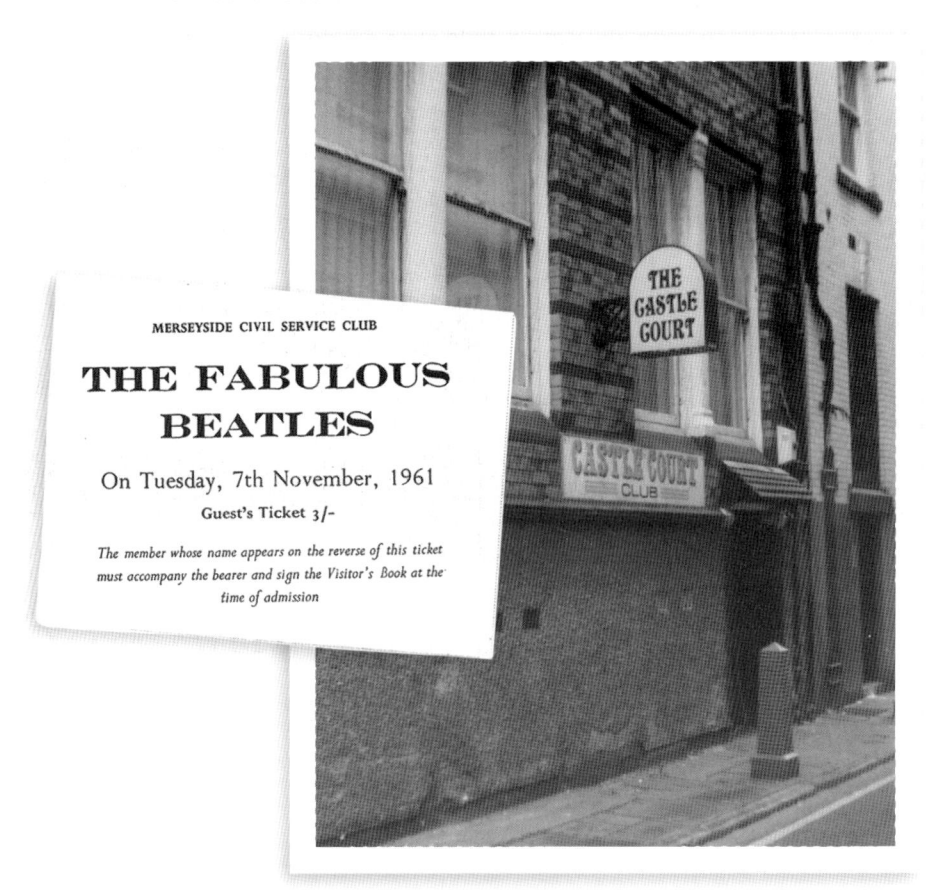

MERSEYSIDE CIVIL SERVICE CLUB

THE FABULOUS BEATLES

On Tuesday, 7th November, 1961

Guest's Ticket 3/-

The member whose name appears on the reverse of this ticket must accompany the bearer and sign the Visitor's Book at the time of admission

MERSEY VIEW
OVERTON HILLS, FRODSHAM, CHESHIRE

Approximately 18 miles from Liverpool, the view from the club offers panoramic views across the Mersey and surrounding area. The Beatles performed here on 20 April 1963, just two days after their appearance at the Royal Albert Hall in a live performance for BBC Radio for a programme called 'Swing Sound 63' alongside, and amongst others, Del Shannon and Kenny Lynch. Following this broadcast, Paul met Jane Asher, with whom he was romantically involved for a number of years. Today, the Mersey View is known as The View and is still an extremely popular entertainment venue, particularly at weekends. The Crickets played here in March 1991. It is two miles from the delightful village of Frodsham, which is well worth a visit in its own right.

MORETON CO-OPERATIVE HALL
366 HOYLAKE ROAD, MORETON, WIRRAL

In 1961, The Beatles played at two venues in Liverpool whose premises were owned by the Co-operative Society: Blair Hall in Walton and Holyoake Hall close to Penny Lane. In the same year, they also appeared at branch number 60 of the society in Moreton, which was sited on the busy Hoylake Road. The first floor of the building boasted a large dance and entertainment area. This was one of three venues that they appeared at in Moreton. As The Quarry Men, they appeared at the Haig Hall Club in 1957 and, in 1962, The Beatles made one appearance at the Apollo Roller Rink. No longer owned by the Co-operative, the building, now known as Carlton House, has changed little externally from the time The Beatles and other bands appeared there.

THE MORGUE
25 OAKHILL PARK, 'BALGOWNIE' BROADGREEN, LIVERPOOL 13

'Balgownie' was owned by Mrs Thompson, the aunt of Alan Caldwell, who was better known as Rory Storm. She had two teenage daughters who had persuaded her to let them use the cellar as a club for their friends. It could accommodate approximately 100 people but had only the basic facilities and its life as a club was short-lived. Alan, who lived nearby at 54 Broadgreen Road, had his own group – Al Caldwell's Texans – and they, together with The Quarry Men, played at the opening night on 13 March 1959. Ringo Starr joined the band on 25 March 1959 and Alan later adopted the stage name Rory Storm, his Texans becoming the Hurricanes. The club finally closed on 22 April 1959 on police advice. It has been written that George Harrison first played with The Quarry Men on the opening night, although this is felt to be apocryphal. However, it is known that the young George made several visits to the club to watch the various bands perform, including The Quarry Men, having formed a friendship with Paul McCartney at school.

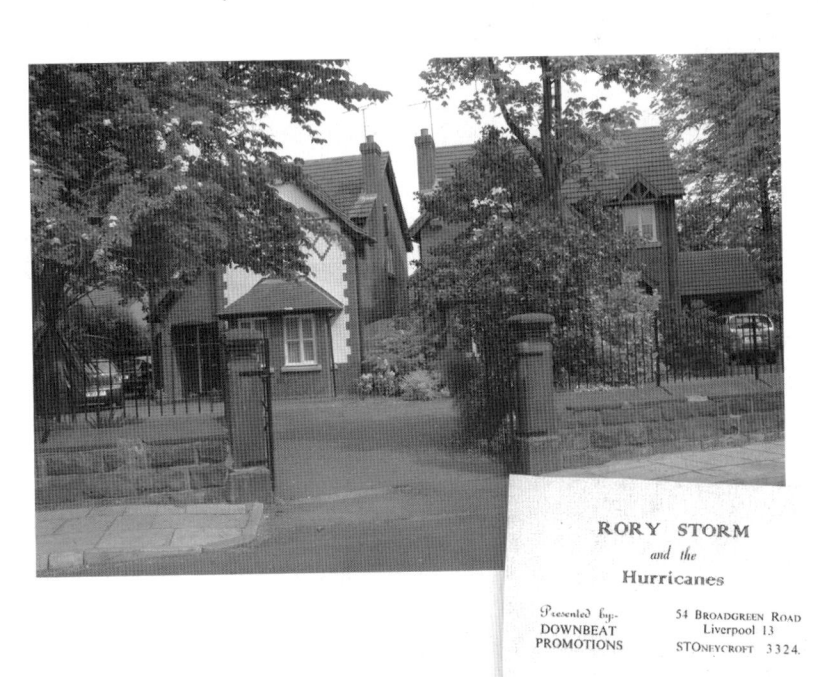

RORY STORM
and the
Hurricanes

Presented by:-
DOWNBEAT
PROMOTIONS

54 BROADGREEN ROAD
Liverpool 13
STOneycroft 3324

MOSSWAY HALL
MOSSWAY, CROXTETH, LIVERPOOL 11

The Beatles appeared here on St Patrick's night, 17 March 1961, an engagement promoted by an organisation called Ivamar, who also put on shows at St Luke's Hall in Crosby, also known as the Jive Hive, and at the Ivamar club in Skelmersdale. The Quarry Men did make a single appearance at the Jive Hive but there is no record of The Beatles in any guise performing in Skelmersdale. Immediately on completing their set at Mossway Hall, they proceeded to the Iron Door club for their second engagement that evening. The original Mossway Hall was demolished and a new building now stands on the site.

MPTE SOCIAL CLUB
FINCH LANE, LIVERPOOL 14

Situated on the corner of Finch Lane and East Prescot Road, its full title was the Liverpool Corporation Passenger Transport Employees' Social and Athletic Club. It was one of several social clubs in Liverpool for employees of the bus services and George Harrison's father, Harold, was for a while social secretary, responsible for organising events. He used his influence to obtain bookings for The Quarry Men, including one appearance here in 1959. He had told George that the manager of the local Pavilion cinema would be in the audience with a view to booking the band for a future engagement but, unfortunately, it all went horribly wrong. It is alleged that John and Paul got drunk during the interval and the second half of the show was a disaster. Some historians have cited this as the occasion on which Colin Hanton was so annoyed with this behaviour that he walked out on the group, never to return, although others mention other venues. Long demolished, a private housing development now occupies the site.

MV ROYAL IRIS
RIVER MERSEY

Synonymous with Liverpool's heyday, The Royal Iris proudly sailed the River Mersey as a cruise ship and floating restaurant, a symbol of the happy and carefree days of the 1950s and 1960s. She was built for Wallasey Corporation in 1951 and withdrawn in 1990 for static use, initially in Liverpool, later in Swansea and sadly was left languishing in a dilapidated state on the banks of the River Thames. The Beatles made four appearances on the Iris as it sailed up and down the River during a series of events known as Riverboat Shuffles. It was also affectionately known as The Fish and Chip Boat due to the sale of that great British institution on board. The four hour jaunt would start and end at the Pier Head. They first appeared on 25 August 1961, sharing a bill with Acker Bilk, and their final appearance was 28 September 1962 with Lee Castle and the Barons.

NEW BRIGHTON PROMENADE PIER
NEW BRIGHTON, WIRRAL

Built in 1867, adjacent to the ferry pier on the north side, it was 550 feet long and 70 feet wide. The whole structure of the pier was rebuilt in 1931 at a cost of £45,000 and access to it was either from its own entrance on the promenade, or direct from the ferry boat. During its lifetime, it played host to a wide variety of entertainment and, in the early sixties, many bands from the Merseyside area and beyond, including The Beatles, appeared here. Bob Evans recalls Ringo Starr lugging his drum kit along the pier at the end of one particular show. Unfortunately, this engagement, or previous ones, have not been recorded, although Pete Best clearly remembers playing at the pier in 1960 and 1961. Sadly, it was demolished in 1978, the ferry pier suffering the same fate some five years earlier due to problems with the sand preventing boats berthing at low water and a rapid decline in passengers. The last boat sailed from New Brighton on 26 September 1971. In 1953, almost 3 million people sailed to New Brighton but, by the early seventies, the figure was only 300,000. However, at the time of writing, there are moves afoot to reintroduce the ferry service from Liverpool to New Brighton.

NEW CABARET ARTISTES CLUB
174A UPPER PARLIAMENT STREET, LIVERPOOL 8

In 1959 and 1960, the cellar of this large Victorian house was used as a strip club by Lord Woodbine and Allan Williams. At this time, The Silver Beetles were desperate for any sort of work and they gladly accepted Williams' offer of ten shillings each for two, 25-minute spots a night. They had the dubious honour of backing the infamous stripper Janice, and Paul recalls their embarrassment when she turned to face them. Not surprising really, because Paul was still a pupil at the nearby Institute when they appeared here in the early months of 1960! At the time, strip clubs were illegal in Liverpool, although many existed in this particular area of the city. It was in 1981 that the street would earn world-wide notoriety for its involvement in the Toxteth riots. Long demolished, the club was situated on the corner of Upper Parliament Street and Kimberly Street.

NEW CLUBMOOR HALL (CONSERVATIVE CLUB)
BROADWAY, LIVERPOOL 11

The Quarry Men made three appearances at this venue and the first, on 18 October 1957, was highly significant, for it was Paul McCartney's debut with the band. By all accounts it was not a success, as he played lead guitar for the one and only time and ruined his version of Arthur Smith's 1946 hit, 'Guitar Boogie'. Admission to this historic event was 15 pence and there were about a hundred paying customers present. Dance promoter Charlie McBain had been responsible for the booking and he at least must have been reasonably impressed as he booked them for two further appearances at the club. He was known as Charlie Mac and ran regular rock and skiffle nights at such venues as Wilson Hall in Garston and Holyoake Hall in Wavertree.

NEW COLONY CLUB
80 BERKELEY STREET, LIVERPOOL 8

Run by Lord Woodbine, known in the local community as Woodie, The Beatles made a couple of informal afternoon session appearances in the cellar of this large terraced property, which was not far from the Rialto Ballroom where they performed twice in 1962. Their appearances at the New Colony occurred sometime in 1960, although exact dates have not been recorded, but it coincided with a time when they would accept any type of work. Much of Berkeley Street has been demolished, including this property, although the magnificent St Nicholas Greek Orthodox Church stands majestically amidst the surrounding squalor. The area is now showing signs of regeneration.

ODD SPOT CLUB
89 BOLD STREET, LIVERPOOL 1

The Odd Spot opened on 9 December 1961 and The Beatles made the first of their two appearances here on 29 March 1962, when they wore suits on stage for only the second time. They had worn them for the first time just five days previously at the Barnston Women's Institute. Brian Epstein arranged for publicity photographs to be taken of the band whilst on stage at the Odd Spot. Their final appearance at the club was on 11 August that year. The club tended to attract teenagers from the more upmarket suburbs of the city and had a smart eating area on the ground floor, whilst the entertainment took place in the rather narrow basement. Situated at No 83 Bold Street was Kaye's Photographers, who took some of the earliest pictures of the band shortly after Ringo joined the line-up.

ODEON CINEMA
GLODDEATH AVENUE, LLANDUDNO, NORTH WALES

Described as the 'Naples of the North' due to its spectacular bay location, Llandudno is a much more genteel resort than its rather brash neighbour, Rhyl, 20 miles down the coast. It does, however, boast a strong musical tradition and, in the late nineteenth century, there were numerous places of entertainment The Beatles performed at the town's Odeon Cinema on six consecutive nights, Monday 12 August – Saturday 17 August 1963, on a bill which also featured Billy J Kramer and the Dakotas and Tommy Quickly. Brian Epstein had high hopes for Quickly but he failed to make the big time. Following their Tuesday evening show, The Beatles returned to Liverpool for one night as they had an appointment the following morning at Granada Studios in Manchester to record two programmes for the North West's topical show 'Scene at 6.30'. Whilst in Llandudno, they stayed at the Grand Hotel situated on the promenade pier. The Odeon had opened in 1934 as the Winter Gardens before changing its name to the Odeon and it then became the Astra. It was demolished in the late 1980s and luxury apartments now occupy the site. Billy Connolly was the last person to perform at the Astra before its closure.

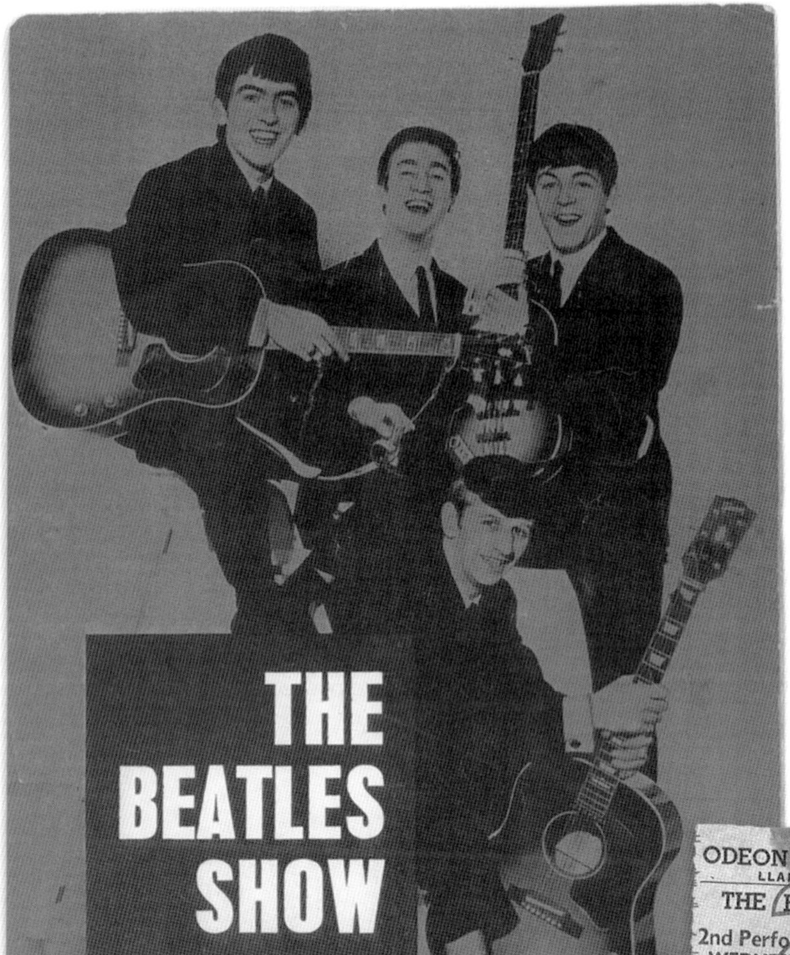
THE
BEATLES
SHOW

ODEON THEATRE
LLANDUDNO
THE BEATLES
2nd Performance 8-50
WEDNESDAY
AUGUST 14
STALLS
6/6
B14
RIGHT
No Tickets exchanged nor money refunded
TO BE RETAINED

ODEON CINEMA
LONDON ROAD, LIVERPOOL 3

The Odeon, formerly the Paramount, was opened in 1934 and was hailed as the last word in picture house entertainment. It boasted a capacity of 2,760 and the first film shown was Cleopatra, starring Claudette Colbert, with music provided by Teddy Joyce and his band. The Beatles made just one live appearance here on 7 December 1963. Earlier in the day, they had participated in two shows for the BBC, 'Juke Box Jury' and 'It's The Beatles' at the nearby Empire Theatre. They then made their way along Pudsey Street, which was a sea of fans wanting to see their idols. The Odeon was the venue for the première of 'Hard Day's Night' on 10 July 1964. In 1984, the Odeon was again selected for the northern première of Paul's film, 'Give My Regards to Broad Street'. Earlier in the day of 28 November, he had been at the Town Hall to receive the Freedom of the City at a special awards ceremony. In 1994, the film 'Backbeat', which charts the band's early career, was given its world première at the Odeon.

ODEON CINEMA
LORD STREET, SOUTHPORT

Opened 3 January 1914 as a cinema called the Palladium with seating for 1,500, it showed films only on Sundays, and was used as a theatre during the week, attracting many of the top stars of the day. In 1929, it suffered severe fire damage and a new 2,120 super cinema was built and, in 1939, its name was changed to the Gaumont. It eventually became the Odeon in 1962 and the following year The Beatles appeared for six consecutive nights, 26-31 August, as part of the Helen Shapiro tour. From Tuesday to Friday during the day, the band were kept busy filming a documentary for the BBC at various locations in the North West, including the nearby Little Theatre. The Odeon closed in 1979, the last film shown being 'Confessions of a Pop Performer'. The building was eventually demolished in 1980 and a supermarket now stands on the site.

PAVILION THEATRE
LODGE LANE, LIVERPOOL 8

A former music hall and striptease theatre, The Beatles made one appearance on 2 April 1962, sharing a bill with the Irish Royal Waterford Showband. The Quarry Men had also performed here in a skiffle contest in the late fifties. In 1956, Lonnie Donegan performed a solo spot and sang his major hit of the time, 'Rock Island Line' which was to have a major influence on budding musicians, including a young Paul McCartney who was in the audience. Known locally as 'The Pivvy', the building became a snooker hall, but more recently has catered for bingo. It was the regional office of the giant Mecca organisation.

PAVILION LODGE LANE
PHONE ROYal 5931

ON STAGE FOR
ONE NIGHT ONLY
MONDAY, 2nd APRIL

COMMENCING 7-30 ———— DOORS OPEN 7 P.M.
FLYING VISIT OF "IRELAND'S PRIDE"!!
THE ROYAL SHOW BAND
(WATERFORD)

Winners of the Carl-Alan Award for the outstanding Showband of the year

ALSO—"MERSEYSIDE'S JOY"
THE BEATLES!!
LIVERPOOL'S OWN BEAT GROUP

All Seats bookable. Prices from 3/6 to 7/6
Box Office open 10 a.m. to 5 p.m. Daily

A NIGHT YOU MUST NOT MISS

PHILLIPS RECORDING STUDIO
38 KENSINGTON, LIVERPOOL 7

Percy Phillips, already an electronics engineer, started a recording business in 1955 which was situated in the middle living room of his terraced family home, having spent £400 on the appropriate equipment. The first group he recorded was Hank Walters and the Dusty Road Ramblers. In the late fifties and early sixties most of the aspiring skiffle and later rock and roll bands recorded here, including Gerry Marsden, The Remo Quartet, The Searchers and The Merseybeats. Bob Wooler used to send bands to Phillips as it was the only place you could make a demonstration record. Phillips also recorded all of Ken Dodd's tapes, which Ken used so he could criticise himself! On 12 July 1958, The Quarry Men paid 17^s 6^d (87.5 pence) to record two numbers: 'That'll Be The Day' and 'In Spite Of All The Danger'. Performing at the session as well as John, Paul and George were Colin Hanton and John 'Duff' Lowe. It was Lowe who kept the original recording. Phillips used to wipe the master tapes to reuse them and save money, little realising how much he could have made if he had kept this particular recording! Paul McCartney eventually bought the tape from Lowe for an undisclosed fee in the early eighties. An acetate was also produced at Phillips of 'Some Other Guy' and 'Beautiful Dreamer' after an audition at Decca. Percy Phillips was 62 years of age when he recorded The Quarry Men and died at the age of 88 in 1984.

P. F. PHILLIPS
38 KENSINGTON,
LIVERPOOL.
NOT TO BE PUBLICLY PERFORMED WITHOUT LICENCE
PRIVATE RECORDING SERVICE
SOME OTHER GUY.
BEAUTIFUL DREAMER.
THE BEATLES
45RPM
Phillips Sound Recording Service
PERSONAL DISCS CUT IN STUDIO OR FROM
— CUSTOMERS TAPES —
38 KENSINGTON, LIVERPOOL 7
Telephone: ANField 5297

PLAZA BALLROOM
DUKE STREET, ST HELENS

The Beatles made five appearances at this venue, the first of which was on 25 June 1962, for which they received a fee of £25. By the time they made their final appearance on 4 March 1963, the fee had quadrupled – their first £100 payment. The Plaza was part of the Whetstone Entertainment Group, who also promoted dances at the Orrell Park Ballroom in Liverpool and the Riverpark Ballroom in Chester. In the late fifties, the Plaza commenced featuring beat groups, and most of the Liverpool bands appeared here, including: The Fourmost, The Searchers, The Merseybeats and The Swinging Bluejeans. The ballroom was open four evenings a week – Friday to Monday – and usually featured three or four groups per night.

PRESCOT CABLES SOCIAL CLUB
HOPE STREET, PRESCOT

Taking its name from the local factory, the amateur soccer club was founded in 1921 and provided a social club for the team and its supporters. The social club, which was situated inside the grounds, started booking beat groups in the late fifties on Saturday and Sunday evenings. The Quarry Men appeared here in 1959 and it has been stated that this was the occasion that Colin Hanton left the group following a dispute with John and Paul, although other venues have been mentioned. Stuart Sutcliffe, whose family lived in nearby Huyton, attended Prescot Grammar School from September 1951 to July 1956. He enlisted at Liverpool College of Art in September 1956, where he would soon encounter John Lennon for the first time.

QUARRY BANK HIGH SCHOOL
HARTHILL ROAD, LIVERPOOL 18

Quarry Bank was John Lennon's senior school from September 1952. It was at the school that The Quarry Men made what was almost certainly their first ever live performance. Ernest Pobjoy allowed the newly formed band to play at a school dance and Colin Lewis, along with other students, organised the event in October 1956. He recalls approaching John whom he had heard had recently formed a skiffle group, to play in the interval. He vividly remembers them being paid ten shillings for their 30-minute spot. The main objective of the school dances was to mingle with the girls at Calder High, which was only divided from Quarry Bank by a wall, which, nevertheless, had the same effect as the Berlin Wall! One of the city's leading grammar schools, it was divided into five houses, with John belonging to Woolton house. Despite his eagerness at the time to leave the establishment, he must have had some fond memories, as in the late seventies he asked Aunt Mimi to send him his old school tie!

Lennon's first gig

THE serialisation of Hunter Davies's book The Quarrymen (News Review, March 25 and last week) was very interesting, but I may be able to fill in one gap. Each year the students at the boys' school Quarry Bank organised a dance around autumn half term, with the objective of meeting the girls at Calder High, a school divided from it by only a wall, which, nevertheless, had the same effect as the Berlin Wall.

It was the responsibility of the lower sixth to organise the event, and in October 1956, I, along with my fellow students, took that responsibility. At that time rock'n'roll and skiffle were just making their presence felt and the usual dance band was likely to be not too exciting. At our pre-event meeting, it was reported that John Lennon, a fifth-former, had started a skiffle group and it was decided that he would be asked to play in the interval when the band went for a few beers.

On the night John, and two others, one of whom I think was Pete Shotton, played using, as I recall, washboard, tea chest and guitar.

I can't remember whether they were any good — apparently they were not, but I can recall vividly the cost. Each of the three members was paid 10 shillings for their half-hour show.

Colin Lewis
Liverpool

QUEEN'S HALL
VICTORIA ROAD, WIDNES, CHESHIRE

The first of five appearances by The Beatles at this venue, approximately 12 miles from Liverpool City Centre, was on 3 September 1962 in a rather hostile environment due to the recent sacking of Pete Best. To complicate matters, they shared the bill with Rory Storm and the Hurricanes, Ringo Starr's previous band. They then appeared the following week – 10 September – again supported by Rory Storm. On 22 October, the other bands on the bill were The Merseybeats and Lee Curtis and the All Stars, who included Pete Best in their ranks and, allegedly, The Beatles totally ignored him. Their final appearance was on 18 February 1963 when they played before two sell-out houses. As well as The Beatles, many top acts have performed at Queen's Hall, including George Melly, The Stone Roses, Johnny Vegas and Bob Geldof. Previously a place of religious worship and opened as a theatre in 1957, this impressive building comprises a main hall and two smaller studio rooms. In recent times, the building has been threatened with closure but, at the time of writing, it is still in active use for various events which include a wide range of concerts and community activities for adults and children.

QUEEN'S HOTEL
THE PROMENADE, SOUTHPORT

Situated on the ground floor of this residential hotel was a jazz club named Club Django after a jazz musician of that name. It featured mainly jazz bands but because of The Beatles' rising popularity, the organisers decided after some heated debate to book them. They made just one appearance on 6 December 1962 and went down well. Directly opposite the Floral Hall theatre, the Queen's was a very popular venue for the theatre-goers who used it for pre-concert, intermission and after-show drinks, as in those days it had a late licence. Sadly, this fine building lay derelict for a number of years but has now been redeveloped and is called the Queen's Hotel Court which provides luxury retirement apartments for the over sixties.

REGENT DANSETTE BALLROOM
HIGH STREET, RHYL, NORTH WALES

This was The Beatles' first engagement in Wales and it took place on 14 July 1962. Tickets for the dance, which commenced at 8pm and finished at 11.30pm, were 5/- (25 pence). Also appearing on the bill were The Strangers another Liverpool band who had appeared with The Beatles at the Aintree Institute in the so-called 'Battle of the Groups', a contest organised by Bob Wooler, and won by The Beatles. Although they never made the big time, The Strangers were a popular local band whose lead singer, Joe Fagin, would go on to have a huge hit in 1984 with 'That's Livin' Alright'. The Regent was situated like many other similar establishments of the time above a branch of Burtons tailors which is still trading, although the Regent is long closed. The Beatles would return to Rhyl almost a year to the day for two sell-out shows at the Ritz Ballroom, by which time they had topped the charts with their third single, 'From Me To You'. Some charts had placed their second single, 'Please Please Me' at number one, but 'From Me To You' is officially recognised as their first UK chart topper.

RIALTO BALLROOM
UPPER PARLIAMENT STREET, STANHOPE STREET, LIVERPOOL 8

Opened as a super cinema and ballroom named the Gaumont-British Rialto Ballroom on 7 October 1927, it was a very popular venue for dinner dances in the thirties and forties. In the late fifties, beat groups started appearing, including The Quarry Men in skiffle contests. The Beatles made two appearances in September and October 1962. The September engagement was a Sam Leach promotion, whilst the October booking was organised by Liverpool University and billed as a 'Rock and Twist Carnival' and also featured The Merseybeats, The Undertakers and Billy Kramer and The Coasters. The Ballroom closed in the late sixties and became a furniture warehouse called Swainbanks. The building was destroyed during riots in 1981. A building of the same name now stands on the site catering for local community needs.

THE RITZ BALLROOM
WEST PARADE, THE PROMENADE, RHYL, NORTH WALES

The Beatles played for two consecutive nights at the ballroom situated on the promenade of this Welsh seaside resort. In the early sixties, it was the most popular dance hall on the North Wales coast. Many bands from Liverpool played here including Farons Flamingos. This was The Beatles' second appearance in the town, having made their debut a year earlier at the Regent Ballroom, about half a mile away. Both concerts at the Ritz on 19 and 20 July 1963 were sell-outs as, by now, they were sweeping all before them in Britain. Tickets for the concerts cost 17/6 (87.5 pence) each night. On 18 July, they had been at EMI in London for a recording session for their second album, taping four songs, 'Till There Was You', 'Money', 'You Really Got A Hold On Me' and 'Devil In Her Heart'. The Ritz was demolished many years ago and part of the Ocean Beach Fun Fair now stands on the site.

RIVERPARK BALLROOM
LOVE STREET, CHESTER

The ballroom was situated on the Grosvenor Park side of the road junction at Union Street and Love Street. It was originally the Kings Arms public house but, in the 1920s, it became the Grosvenor Roller Skating Rink. It then converted to a dance hall called the Broadway Academy of Dance, hence it is still remembered by some people today as the 'Ac'. Named the Riverpark from the forties onwards, it was an extremely popular dancing venue catering for each trend of the day from the big bands to the Merseysound of The Beatles era. The Beatles made four appearances on Thursday evenings in August and September 1962, the first two not without significance. Their first on 16 August was the day of Pete Best's departure and Johnny Hutchison of The Big Three stood in on drums. The following week, John Lennon had married Cynthia earlier in the day but still appeared with the band in the evening! The Grosvenor was demolished in the mid-sixties to accommodate the Chester inner ring road, although the sandstone pillar on the right-hand side of the picture can still be seen today.

76 ROSEBERY STREET
LIVERPOOL 8

The city of Liverpool celebrated the 750th anniversary of King John granting the township a Royal Charter on 22 June 1957 and street parties took place all over the city. One such was held in Rosebery Street and The Quarry Men were engaged to provide some of the entertainment.
Mrs Marjorie Roberts was the main organiser and her son Charles was a friend of Colin Hanton, the group's drummer. A lorry for The Quarry Men to perform on was supplied by Fred Tyrer, who lived at No 76, and it was stationed outside his house. After they had finished playing, they were threatened by some local youths from nearby Hatherley Street, who considered them to be posh kids from Woolton. They sought refuge in Mrs Roberts' house at No 84 before being escorted to the bus stop by a local policeman. Rosebery Street won the prize for the best decorated street in the city and, at that time, it was a thriving community with 160 dwellings. Today it is a scene of desolation and boarded-up properties.

ROYAL LIDO BALLROOM
CENTRAL BEACH, PRESTATYN, NORTH WALES

The Beatles hold the distinction of being the first band from Merseyside to have played at this prestigious venue, which had been opened by the Duke of Kent in June 1960. Pride of place was the ballroom's magnificent maple wood dance floor. They appeared on 24 November 1962, their only engagement here, the booking having been made by Joe Flannery, a close friend of Brian Epstein and brother of singer Lee Curtis. A Liverpool agent, he handled some of the bookings for NEMS enterprises and The Beatles were the first group he booked at the Royal Lido. They received £30 for their two-hour set. Flannery later booked into this venue amongst others, Billy Kramer and the Coasters and Lee Curtis and the All Stars with Pete Best on drums. During the Second World War, many families from Liverpool were evacuated to Prestatyn, including the Epsteins, and it was also here that Neil Aspinall, who would become The Beatles' road manager, was born. In 1990, the Royal Lido underwent a major refurbishment and was renamed the Nova Centre, providing a host of leisure activities and is particularly popular in the summer season.

ROYALTY THEATRE
CITY ROAD, CHESTER

The Royalty was built in 1874 and many leading artistes of the day appeared there. In 1957, the theatre was partly reconstructed and two new cantilever balconies were added. In the early sixties, many top bands appeared including the Rolling Stones and Herman's Hermits. On 15 May 1963, The Beatles, sharing a bill with Gerry and the Pacemakers, played before two houses at 6.30pm and 8.40pm with tickets priced at 30 pence for each performance. This was one of only two venues which The Beatles played in Chester, the other being the Riverpark Ballroom. In the late sixties, to generate extra income, a nightclub was created beneath the stalls area named the Warren Club, changing its name in the seventies to Champers, then Blimpers and most recently the Alchemy. The actual theatre had been derelict since the mid-seventies and, with the nightclub, was eventually demolished in 2003.

STARLINE CLUB
WINDSOR STREET, LIVERPOOL 8

The club formed part of a former cinema, the Warwick Picture Drome, which stood on the corner of Windsor Street and Upper Warwick Street. The Beatles would frequent the premises in the afternoon, following lunchtime sessions at the Cavern, as it was licensed to sell alcohol. They also used the club for rehearsing and, in 1961, performed there in the evenings, although no actual dates have been recorded. The club was also frequented by other bands including The Chants and Gerry and the Pacemakers. The building was demolished in the 1970s. This is the area of the city where Ringo was born and raised. He lived for his first six years at 9 Madryn Street, before moving to 10 Admiral Grove where his 21st Birthday party was held. Health permitting, he attended St Silas Church of England Primary School and then Dingle Vale Secondary Modern. His mother was for a short while a barmaid at the Empress Public House in High Park Street, which features on the album sleeve of Ringo's first solo LP, 'Sentimental Journey'.

ST ALOYSIUS YOUTH CLUB
TWIG LANE, HUYTON, NORTH LIVERPOOL

The Quarry Men appeared at this church youth club in September 1957, one of their earliest recorded bookings. Huyton figures prominently in Beatles history with nearby Hambleton Hall a regular venue for the band in the early 1960s. Stuart Sutcliffe, the so-called fifth Beatle, is buried at nearby Huyton Parish Church graveyard in the 1939 section, number 552. Paul held his 21st birthday party at his Auntie Jin's house, 147 Dinas Lane, which was the infamous occasion when John hospitalised Bob Wooler after he had allegedly questioned his sexuality following his recent holiday with Brian Epstein. The story made the national press and Brian ordered John to issue a formal apology which appeared in the Daily Mirror, the only national paper to report the incident.

ST BARNABUS CHURCH HALL
PENNY LANE, LIVERPOOL 18

Alby and the Sorrals were the resident band at this venue, known locally as Barneys, from October 1961 to March 1963. It was a very popular venue and rival to the nearby Holyoake Hall. Full house signs were a regular occurrence and it hosted many of the top Merseyside bands and some from Manchester. However, the two people who ran it baulked at The Beatles required fee of £15 and refused to book them. When they tried some time later, Brian Epstein was on the scene and the fee had gone up to £25! However, The Quarry Men did perform here in 1957. In 1979, the building was used for the filming of 'The Birth of The Beatles' as the location for the Wyvern Club/Larry Parnes audition of 1960. This impressive building is now called Dovedale Towers. Both John and George attended the nearby Dovedale Road Primary school and also close by is 9 Newcastle Road, where John lived for the first five years of his life before moving to Mendips to be cared for by his Uncle George and Aunt Mimi.

ST EDWARD'S CATHOLIC COLLEGE
SANDFIELD PARK, WEST DERBY, LIVERPOOL 12

Liverpool's oldest and most prestigious Catholic College was the somewhat unusual setting for a Beatles engagement, but they appeared here at a Sunday evening dance on 8 October 1961. Unfortunately, all college records of their appearance have been destroyed, but I have spoken to several people who can recall the event, including the late Bob Azurdia who was an ex-pupil at the college. Bob was one of the first presenters at Radio Merseyside and interviewed The Beatles on a couple of occasions. He recalled Paul singing 'Besame Mucho' at St Edward's, which went down well, in contrast to their more raucous numbers which were not well received. They were not rebooked! For Pete Best, this booking was more or less on his doorstep, with the Casbah little more than half a mile away. The college is situated in one of Liverpool's most exclusive settings and is little changed from the days that The Beatles played there.

ST JOHN'S CHURCH HALL
SNAEFELL AVENUE, TUEBROOK, LIVERPOOL 13

The Beatles made 11 appearances at this small suburban venue, all in 1961. For their first booking on 17 February they received a £20 fee – an unusually large amount at this time. Pete Best's mother made this booking and others in 1961 and 1962, acting in an unofficial capacity as manager and agent. She promoted them under the name of Casbah Promotions and obtained engagements for them at several other local venues, as well as her own Casbah Club in nearby West Derby. St John's had a very forward-thinking curate at this time, who saw the value of holding beat sessions at the hall for the local youths, rather than them spending their time on street corners with little to do. As well as The Beatles, other local bands and singers who appeared here included The Big Three and Cilla Black.

ST JOHN'S HALL
ORIEL ROAD, BOOTLE

David Forshaw was a 17-year-old promoter who, with fellow promoter Brian Kelly, gained entrance to The Beatles' dressing room at Litherland Town Hall on 27 December 1960 and promptly booked them for three dates at St John's, the first of which was on 6 January 1961, for which they received a fee of £6.10s (£6.50). In total, they would make five appearances at this venue. Their final appearance was on 30 July 1962, by which time David Forshaw had given the hall its own name, the Blue Penguin Club. St John's Hall, opposite Bootle Town Hall, was also the premises of the local Conservative Association. Now long demolished, many leading Merseyside bands appeared here, including The Remo Four and The Merseybeats. The Merseybeats had a Monday night residency at the hall and, at the time, were one of Merseyside's most popular bands and are still performing today.

ST LUKE'S HALL
96 LIVERPOOL ROAD, CROSBY, LIVERPOOL 23

Better known as the Jive Hive the resident band was Ian and the Zodiacs who earned a respectable £3.10s (£3.50) a night at this small suburban hall. At this stage of their career, in common with some other groups, they preferred to earn a regular income in the suburbs rather than branch out into the city centre where work was uncertain. The Quarry Men made a single appearance here in November 1957. Most of the other Liverpool bands also performed at this popular venue, although there is no record of The Beatles appearing. Now called the Comrades Club, it has been transformed into a social club and inside bears little resemblance to the original dance hall, although it is still used periodically as a dance venue when some of the original Mersey groups play at nostalgia evenings.

ST PAUL'S PRESBYTERIAN CHURCH HALL
NORTH ROAD, TRANMERE, BIRKENHEAD, WIRRAL

The Beatles made two appearances at this venue, firstly on 10 February 1962 when on the previous evening they had performed at the Technical College, less than a quarter of a mile away. Their second and final appearance at St Paul's was on 10 March when they were joined on the bill by The Country Four with Brian Newman. Tickets cost 5/- (25 pence) and The Beatles received a £20 fee, plus their travel costs through the Mersey Tunnel on Brian Epstein's insistence. To give an insight into the band's work-rate at this stage in their career, this was their 29th day of bookings without a break, which included a couple of occasions playing three different venues in one day. It would be another 22 days before they finally got a well-earned rest! St Paul's, which was demolished long ago, stood on the corner of Rocky Bank Road and North Road and private dwellings now occupy the site. It was built in 1900, the same year as the nearby St Joseph's Catholic Church, which is still operational.

ST PETER'S CHURCH GARDEN FÊTE
CHURCH ROAD, WOOLTON, LIVERPOOL 25

The 6 July 1957 is undoubtedly the most significant date in the history of The Beatles. That afternoon, in a field behind the church, The Quarry Men performed at the church's annual garden fête and it was here that a 15-year-old Paul McCartney, having cycled from his home in Allerton, saw John Lennon and his band for the first time. It was not, from all accounts, one of The Quarry Men's better performances, but Paul must have been sufficiently impressed to have gone over the road with his pal Ivan Vaughan to the church hall, where the band were setting up their gear for an evening performance. In 1997, on the 40th anniversary of John and Paul's historic meeting, The Quarry Men reformed and played a set at the garden fête with a plaque being unveiled at the end of a special church service. In his youth, John had been a Sunday School member at St Peter's and attended confirmation classes. The gravestone of Eleanor Rigby is situated in St Peter's graveyard, prompting many theories that Paul or John may have seen it many years earlier and stored it in their sub-conscious. In 1982, Tommy Steele donated a statue of the infamous Eleanor to the city of Liverpool, which is situated in Stanley Street, near to the Cavern Club. Also in Stanley Street was Hessy's musical instrument store where John Lennon bought his first proper guitar in 1957 for £15.

IN LOVING MEMORY OF
MY DEAR HUSBAND
JOHN RIGBY
WHO DEPARTED THIS LIFE
OCT 4TH 1913 AGED 72 YEARS
AT REST.
ALSO FRANCES, WIFE OF THE ABOVE,
DIED APRIL 3RD 1928, AGED 85 YEARS.
ALSO DORIS W. DAUGHTER OF
F & E RIGBY, DIED DEC. 24TH 1927,
AGED 2 YEARS & 3 MONTHS.
ALSO ELEANOR RIGBY

THE PARISH OF
ST. PETER, WOOLTON
SUNDAY SERVICES
STAFF

ST PETER'S CHURCH HALL
CHURCH ROAD, WOOLTON, LIVERPOOL 25

As well as performing at the garden fête on the afternoon of 6 July 1957, The Quarry Men appeared at the church hall in the evening with the exception of Colin Hanton, and it was whilst setting up their gear for the dance, which commenced at 8pm, that John and Paul first met. It was Ivan Vaughan who occasionally played the tea chest bass with the group and was a classmate of Paul's who initiated the introduction. Ivan and Paul had identical dates of birth and were very good friends at the Liverpool Institute and when Ivan tragically died in 1994, having contracted Parkinson's disease when only in his early thirties, Paul, who had kept in contact with him throughout his career, was said to be distraught. The Quarry Men also played on several other unrecorded dates at the hall. The dances would begin at 7.30pm and finish by 10pm. Woolton was John's playground in his youth for, as well as living in the area, he spent a lot of time in nearby Reynolds Park and, of course, Strawberry Field. The church and hall have changed little since the late fifties, although at one time it was proposed to demolish the stage they performed on. Thankfully, this did not occur and an important piece of the band's history has been preserved.

TECHNICAL COLLEGE HALL
BOROUGH ROAD, BIRKENHEAD, WIRRAL

The Beatles played here on three consecutive Fridays in February 1962 at the popular student dances. They were involved in an amusing, if not potentially serious incident at the time, on their final appearance on 23 February 1962. It was not unusual in those days for them to play three, if not four, gigs in one day and this day was no exception. Having played at the Cavern at lunchtime, they were booked in the evening to appear at the Tower Ballroom in New Brighton for two sets at 9pm and 11pm with a 30-minute performance in between at the college. On leaving the college at 10.30pm to return to New Brighton, they discovered that their van had run out of petrol. Fortunately, the college was situated immediately next door to Borough Filling Station, which, although just closing for the night, allowed them to purchase petrol. They made the Tower with just minutes to spare! In later years, the college changed its name to the Wirral Metropolitan College and is directly opposite North Road where another Beatles venue, St Paul's Church Hall, was situated. St Paul's has long since been demolished, the college building was also demolished in May 2005.

THE INSTITUTE
HINDERTON ROAD, NESTON, CHESHIRE

Neston Institute was opened in 1902 as a Liberal Club, at a cost of £3,000 and seated 900. During the First World War, the building was called the Neston Red Cross Hospital and was used to treat wounded soldiers. It was later used for a variety of social activities, including dances. The Silver Beetles made the first of six Thursday night appearances at this venue, situated on the Wirral and Cheshire border on 2 June 1960. This was their second engagement since returning from their tour of Scotland with Johnny Gentle. The shows were promoted by Les Dodd of Paramount Enterprises who was also responsible for similar events at the Grosvenor Ballroom in Wallasey. He had been promoting traditional dances since 1936 and had somewhat reluctantly arrived at the conclusion that rock sessions would be more lucrative. The band were paid £10 between them for each appearance, out of which their agent Allan Williams received £1 commission. Today, the building is little changed, although it is now known as the Civic Hall.

'Rock' group at Neston Institute

A LIVERPOOL rhythm group "The Beatles", made their debut at Neston Institute on Thursday night when north-west promoter, Mr. Les Dodd, presented three-and-a-half hours of rock 'n' roll.

The five-strong group, which has been pulling in capacity houses on Merseyside, comprises three guitars, bass and drums.

John Lennon, the leader, plays one of the three rhythm guitars, the other guitarists being Paul Ramon and Carl Harrison. Stuart Da Stael plays the bass, and the drummer is Thomas Moore. They all sing, either together, or as soloists.

Recently they returned from a Scottish tour, starring Johnny Gentle, and are looking forward to a return visit in a months time.

Among the theatres they have played at are the Hippodrome, Manchester; the Empire, Liverpool and the Pavilion, Aintree.

CIVIC HALL

TOWER BALLROOM
NEW BRIGHTON, WIRRAL

Sam Leach, saw the potential of this vast ballroom and organised a show – Operation Big Beat – featuring five Liverpool bands: Gerry and the Pacemakers, Rory Storm and The Hurricanes, The Remo Four, Kingsize Taylor and the Dominoes and, topping the bill, The Beatles. It took place on 10 November 1961 and commenced at 7.30pm, finishing at 1am. Tickets were 5s (25p) and transport was available through the Mersey tunnel. The Beatles played their first set at 8pm, before fulfilling an engagement at Knotty Ash Village Hall in Liverpool. They then returned to the Tower for their final spot at 11.30pm. The Beatles would appear at the Tower on a staggering 27 occasions. Sam Leach was responsible for a number of the shows, but Bob Wooler and Brian Epstein also staged concerts here. Leach's second Operation Big Beat, on 24 November 1961, attracted the largest crowd ever to witness a Beatles performance on the British mainland, almost 4,000. The Beatles' final appearance was on 14 June 1963 for a NEMS enterprises production entitled, Mersey Beat Showcase, and they were supported by Gerry and The Pacemakers and five other bands. The Tower Ballroom was burned down in 1969. It had originally sported an iron tower, taller than Blackpool's and second only in height to the Eiffel Tower. Dismantling commenced in 1919, taking almost two years for the tower to be removed completely. George Harrison's grandfather was a commissionaire at the Tower in the thirties. In November 2001, a 40th anniversary concert took place as part of a series of events and appropriately called Operation Big Beat at the resort's Floral Pavilion Theatre.

A Bob Wooler SHOW
TOWER
BALLROOM NEW BRIGHTON
NUMBER ONE ... STAR SHOW
LICENSED BARS
THE BEATLES
Parlophone Recording Artistes
HEY! BABY
BRUCE Channel
AND
DELBERT McLINTON
(HARMONICA)
DIRECT from AMERICA!
with The BARONS
THE BIG THREE
THE Statesmen The NORTH'S FABULOUS FIVE!
THE FOUR JAYS
THURSDAY 21ST JUNE · 1962
7·30 TO 12 P.M.
TICKETS 4'6 IN ADVANCE 5'6 ON THE NIGHT
AVAILABLE FROM NEMS · RUSHWORTHS · LEWIS'S · HESSK
STROTHERS Etc. & TOWER BALLROOM
OPERATION
'Big Beat'
TOWER BALLROOM
NEW BRIGHTON
Friday, 10TH Nov. 1961
7·30 P.M. to 1·0 A.M.
★ Rocking to Merseysides TOP 5 GROUPS
The Beatles
Rory Storm and the Hurricanes
Gerry & The Pacemakers
The Remo Four
Kingsize Taylor and the Dominoes
2 LICENSED BARS (until 11·30 P.M.) BUFFET
Special Late Transport (L.POOL · WIRRAL · CHESHIRE)
TICKETS 5/-
from RUSHWORTHS · LEWIS'S
CRANES · STOTHERS
TOWER BALLROOM

TOWN HALL
MARKET STREET, EARLESTOWN, NEWTON-LE-WILLOWS

Following a lunchtime booking at the Cavern on 30 November 1962, The Beatles appeared that evening at this civic building for an engagement billed as 'The Big Beat Show No 2', which was organised by the football section of the T and T Vicars Sports and Social Club. The building is well over one hundred years old and regularly held dances in the sixties. Earlier in the day, mixes of The Beatles' second single 'Please Please Me' and 'Ask Me Why' were produced at Abbey Road by George Martin, although The Beatles were not present.

25 UPTON GREEN
SPEKE, LIVERPOOL 24

The Harrison family left their small terraced house in Wavertree in 1949 and moved to a new council estate in Speke, about five miles away. On 20 December 1958, The Quarry Men played at the wedding reception of George's older brother Harry, which was held in the family home. As a 13-year-old, George had played with his brother Peter at the British Legion Club in Dam Wood Road, Speke, with their band The Rebels, their one and only booking. George apparently loved the wide open spaces of his new surroundings but his mother never really settled and missed the tight-knit community of Wavertree. The Harrison family lived here until 1962, before moving to 174 Mackets Lane, Hunts Cross, where they stayed for 18 months. Speke Airport was the scene of a tumultuous reception when The Beatles returned to their home town for a civic reception and the Northern première of 'A Hard Days Night' in 1964. These days the Airport boasts a new terminal building appropriately named after John Lennon. Paul also lived for a while with his family in Speke, firstly at 72 Western Avenue and then at 12 Ardwick Road, before moving to Forthlin Road in Allerton in 1955. He also attended Stockton Wood Road Primary School in Speke.

VICTORIA HALL
VILLAGE ROAD, HIGHER BEBINGTON, WIRRAL

The Beatles made one appearance here on 4 August 1962. So few bands had played at this venue that Brian Epstein had difficulty locating the hall. John and Paul, though, would have been familiar with the area, as Paul's large family lived close by, whilst John spent many a school holiday with his Aunt Annie in nearby Rock Ferry. In fact, one of his favourite photographs was taken with his mother Julia, in his aunt's back garden. Paul still has family in the area and has been spotted occasionally in recent years enjoying a glass or two in the quaint Travellers Rest hostelry.

WAVERTREE TOWN HALL
89 HIGH STREET, LIVERPOOL 15

Between 1957 and 1959, The Quarry Men made numerous appearances at various social functions, mainly in South Liverpool, arranged for them by friends, exact dates of which have sadly not been preserved. In September 1957, one such booking was at a function at this imposing building. Built in 1872, it originally contained the offices of the Registrar, the Land Office and the Magistrates Court. It was also used for social occasions such as weddings and engagement parties. The Wavertree motto is above the door which translated from the Latin reads, 'I flourish in the shade'. It was closed in 1967 for a while but was refurbished and reopened as a restaurant and bar and it still caters for private functions. Nearby is 12 Arnold Grove, George's birthplace, where he lived for the first six years of his life.

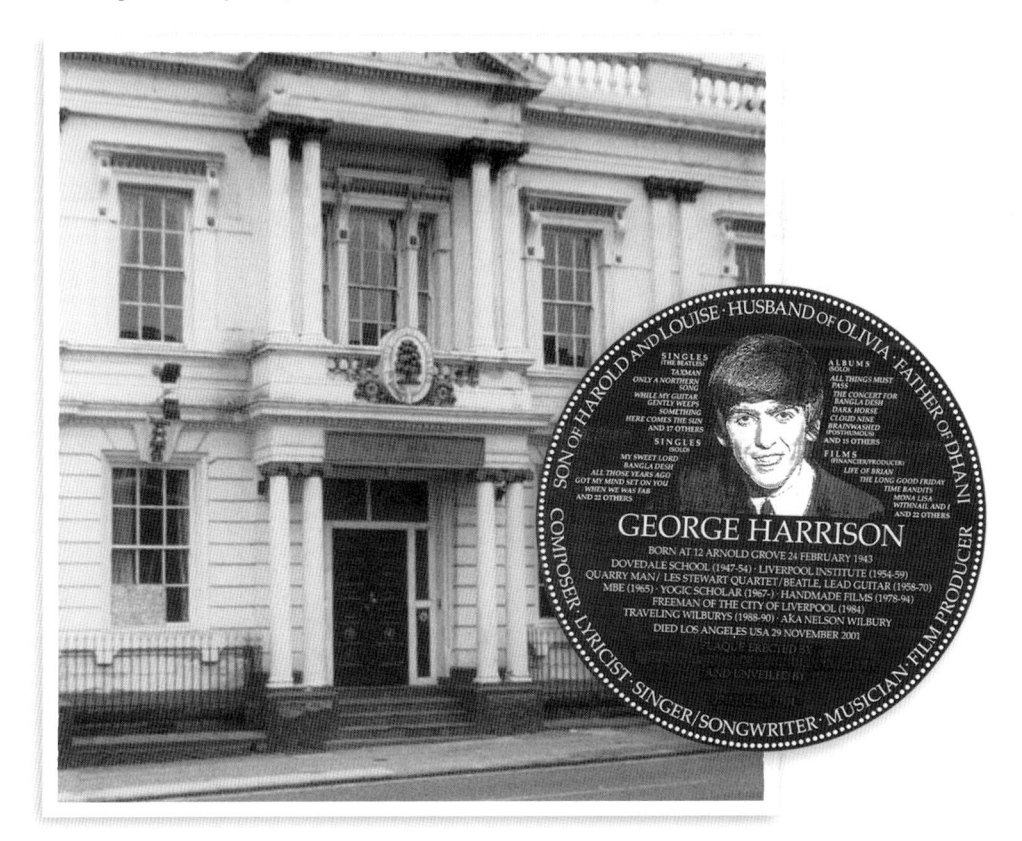

WILSON HALL
SPEKE ROAD, GARSTON, LIVERPOOL 19

Situated on the corner with Tudwal Street, Wilson Hall was a popular venue and featured 'Rhythm Nights' each Thursday, run by Charlie McBain. The Quarry Men made at least four recorded appearances here, three in 1957 and one in 1959, and possibly more on unrecorded dates. It has been stated that George Harrison first met The Quarry Men at Wilson Hall on 6 February 1958 but this has been questioned by some writers. George's mother always maintained that they met at a local fish and chip shop. George's father was responsible for bookings at the nearby Speke Bus Depot Social Club and booked the band for a post-Christmas function at Wilson Hall for the depot's employees on 1 January 1959. Wilson Hall was built by Francis Wilson and, in the seventies, became a supermarket and, in more recent times, a carpet warehouse.

WINTER GARDENS
HEALD STREET, GARSTON, LIVERPOOL 19

The Garston and District Co-operative Society, Cafeteria and Winter Gardens Ballroom was situated immediately adjacent to a Welsh Methodist Chapel and directly opposite a police station. The Quarry Men appeared here in a skiffle contest in 1957, which was a typical engagement at this stage of their career, as most of their appearances then were as hopeful entrants in similar events, usually unpaid and unsuccessful. The Co-operative Society had a number of similar premises in Merseyside which many bands, including The Beatles, performed at, such as Blair Hall, Holyoake Hall and the Moreton Co-op Hall. Garston would have been a very familiar area to the group, as they all lived nearby. John's mother Julia lived at 1 Blomfield Road and, during his early teenage years, it became a second home to him.

WOOLTON VILLAGE CLUB
ALLERTON ROAD, WOOLTON, LIVERPOOL 25

Woolton, approximately seven miles from Liverpool city centre, is rich in Beatles history and attracts many fans, particularly to sites such as St Peter's and Strawberry Field. A much overlooked venue, however, is the local village club, for it was here that The Quarry Men made a single appearance on 24 January 1959. The event was a late Christmas party when they played a ten minute selection of skiffle numbers. The club is still thriving today and is a mere two minute walk from St Peter's.

WYVERN SOCIAL CLUB (BLUE ANGEL)
108 SEEL STREET, LIVERPOOL 1

The Silver Beetles auditioned here on 10 May 1960 for Larry Parnes, a top British promoter of the time, who was seeking a backing band for his Liverpudlian protégé, Billy Fury, who was shortly embarking on a tour of Britain, with a whole array of other top stars including Marty Wilde and Tommy Steele. Parnes had asked Allan Williams to assemble some local bands for audition at a club Williams had recently acquired called the Wyvern and which he would shortly rename the Blue Angel. The other groups present were Cass and the Cassanovas, Gerry and the Pacemakers, Derry and the Seniors and Cliff Roberts and the Rockers. Parnes and Fury were both in attendance. What followed next is open to question, as various myths have been expounded, and I am not going to add to the list other than to say that The Silver Beetles were not chosen, although Parnes enlisted them to accompany another of his stable, Johnny Gentle, who was also from Liverpool, on a forthcoming tour of Scotland. Before setting out on their first ever tour, three of the band decided to adopt stage names. Paul became Paul Ramon, George was Carl Harrison and Stuart Sutcliffe chose Stuart de Stael, presumably after the Russian artist Nicholas de Stael. The tour saw them play seven engagements from 20-28 May 1960. In the sixties, many top musicians including Bob Dylan, The Rolling Stones and Judy Garland would visit the Blue Angel when in Liverpool.

YE CRACKE
13 RICE STREET, LIVERPOOL1

Not a venue as such, but certainly a favourite watering hole of the band, and in particular, of John Lennon. John attended the nearby Art College and spent many an hour in here putting the world to rights, usually in the company of fellow students including Stuart Sutcliffe, Bill Harry and Rod Murray. They were known as the Dissenters and a plaque has been erected inside the Pub as a tribute to them. It was also here that John took Cynthia on their first date. John's antics in the pub are legendary, but one afternoon he went too far, which resulted in him being banned never to return. The author recalls a conversation with the formidable landlady many years later who, in no uncertain terms, indicated that he still would not be allowed back, despite his then world-wide fame! In December 1959, John and Paul sang a couple of numbers in a tiny room in the pub known as the 'War Office', much to the delight of fellow drinkers. Whilst it has changed little externally, the inside has seen major alterations, being extended and walls having been knocked down. No longer the snug little room with a fireplace and a large etching of The Death of Nelson on the wall, where John and his pals used to drink. Well worth a visit though!

YMCA
56–60 WHETSTONE LANE, BIRKENHEAD, WIRRAL

The Young Men's Christian Association had been opened in nearby Grange Road in 1890 and moved to Whetstone Lane on 4 February 1938, the opening ceremony performed by the Earl of Shrewsbury. The YMCA has always provided a wide range of social activities for young people and The Beatles made one appearance here on 8 September 1962 and, following their set, made their way to the Majestic Ballroom in Conway Street, less than a mile away. The Beatles made just one other appearance at a YMCA building, in Hoylake, on 24 February 1962, which has now been demolished, unlike the Birkenhead premises, which externally at least, is little altered.

YMCA
BIRKENHEAD ROAD, HOYLAKE, WIRRAL

The club organiser, Charles Tranter, had been so anxious to book the band that he drove over to Pete Best's home in West Derby with the offer of a £30 fee! They made one appearance at this venue on 24 February 1962, although they were not that well received by the audience and were actually booed off the stage. Conflicting accounts have been cited for this reaction, one being the band's lengthy introductions between numbers and the other the presence in the audience of many Gerry and the Pacemakers fans! Following the show, The Beatles packed up their equipment and departed for a midnight engagement at the Cavern. Long demolished, a private apartment block now stands on the former YMCA site, but a plaque commemorates the site of the original building. Hoylake has numerous Beatles connections. Cynthia Powell, John's first wife, was brought up in the town and lived at 18 Trinity Road and spent a short time in the Cottage Hospital. Julian was christened at the Parish church in Trinity Road which was directly opposite the family home, and he was for a while a pupil at Kingsmead school, where a teacher taught him to play the guitar, prompting John to remark some years later that he regretted not having spent more time with his son and that he should have been the one to teach him to play the instrument. When not on the road, John would spend the occasional night at Trinity Road.

ON THIS SITE STOOD HOYLAKE Y.M.C.A.
FOR MANY YEARS A SOCIAL CENTRE
FOR THE AREA.
HOYLAKE Y.M.C.A. WERE ALL ENGLAND
BASKETBALL CHAMPIONS 1936-37
AND REPRESENTED ENGLAND AT
THE PARIS EXPOSITION 1937.
THIS PLAQUE WAS ERECTED BY FORMER
FRIENDS, RATEPAYERS ASSOC.
AND STIER HOMES
30TH OCTOBER 1987.

OTHER VENUES PLAYED

A definitive guide to all of The Beatles' early venues is impossible, particularly between 1957 and 1959 when, as The Quarry Men, many engagements were not noted down, or advertised. It is known that they did play at several private functions, mainly in South Liverpool, and often for little or no fee, although it is accepted that during this period they did appear at both the Childwall and Lee Park Labour Clubs and Halewood Village Hall. It is also possible that they performed at other venues as late as 1960-61 which were not documented, as it was only after Brian Epstein became their manager in late 1961 that every appearance and payment received was written down. Each venue in this book has been carefully researched, although the author accepts no responsibility for any inaccuracies or omissions.